178
£ 24.99
1/02

Anxiety-Free me

Anxiety-Free Me

My life with anxiety disorders and my recovery from them

CHARLES LINDEN

foreword by
LINDA ROBSON

The information given in this book should not be treated as a substitute for professional medical advice; always consult a medical practitioner. Any use of information in this book is at the reader's discretion and risk. Neither the author nor the publisher can be held responsible for any loss, claim or damage arising out of the use, or misuse, or the suggestions made or the failure to take medical advice.

First published 2014

ISBN 978-0-9927231-4-9

Contents

Dedication

For 'Uncle' David Lane

1947–2008

Your support, guidance and friendship are missed every day!

Foreword

by Linda Robson

A S AN ACTRESS, who's worked in the business for over forty-five years, anxiety has been something I've had to deal with for a very long time.

Anxiety is a normal part of my job.

It's the feeling I get in my stomach before walking into an audition. The butterflies I get before walking on stage in front of thousands of people. The nerves I experience five minutes before appearing on live TV.

To be honest, I don't know anyone in my world that hasn't had to deal with anxiety in some shape or form. Nerves are natural in my world. Nerves are expected when you do what I do.

What I was unaware of is that thousands – if not millions – of people all over the world experience these same feelings of anxiety on a daily basis whilst living their lives. The same feeling I get before performing in front of thousands of people, others experience in the checkout queue in Tesco. The same knot of nerves in my stomach before a live interview, others have whilst riding on the bus. The same rush of adrenaline, which shoots through my body when the director shouts 'ACTION', shoots through their body as they leave the front door.

I was unaware that there were people in the world that suffered with anxiety disorders and panic attacks every day of their lives.

That was, until my son became one of them.

My son was twenty when he suffered his first panic attack.

I'd heard of people having them before and just assumed it was a one-off that would be forgotten and soon everything would be all right. I couldn't have been more wrong and I wasn't prepared for what happened next.

Within days of his first panic attack my son was a prisoner in his own room, as the fear of having another panic attack brought on agoraphobia, OCD (obsessive-compulsive disorder) and acute anxiety.

He locked himself away. He stopped eating. He stopped seeing his friends and couldn't attend his big sister's wedding.

It felt like everything had changed overnight. My son went from a normal, independent young man to someone who couldn't even leave the house without my husband or me being with him. And things only got worse.

We tried everything – doctors, councillors, psychologists, therapists, hypnosis, meditation, EFT (emotional freedom technique) – but nothing seemed to work. If anything it just made his anxiety worse.

After months and months of trying so hard but getting no results we had almost lost hope . . . then we found Charles Linden.

My husband and I stumbled across The Linden Method online and, after reading about Charles and his team and the work they did, I have to admit that, at first, it sounded almost too good to be true. I, once again, couldn't have been more wrong.

After countless doctors trying to persuade us to give our son all sorts of medication, and after every therapist and councillor telling him he would need weekly sessions for the rest of his life, here at last here was a way that didn't claim he would need any of this in order to become anxiety free.

And after countless 'ists', who's understanding of anxiety seemed to go no further than a paragraph in a textbook, here at last was someone who really knew what our son was going through, as he had been through it all, and much worse, himself.

We ordered The Linden Method straight away and after my son read about Charles' experiences and what he had to say about anxiety so we realised that we'd finally found 'the man and the method', which could help us get our lives back.

And now my son's anxiety is nothing more than a memory.

He is not only anxiety free but also living a fuller life than he did before. No more agoraphobia, no more OCD, no more panic attacks. No more bloody anxiety. Our house is back to normal. Our lives are back on track and the future is exciting once again.

We will never be able to thank Charles and his team enough for what they did for us. They are not just life-changers they are lifesavers.

It scares me to think that there are people in this world that are suffering the way my son did – people who feel they have no way out.

Well there is a way out and it's The Linden Method.

You are not alone. You are not helpless and no matter how dark the tunnel in which you've found yourself you will inevitably find the light.

My son is living proof of that.

Linda Robson

About *Anxiety-Free Me*

THIS IS THE STORY of one-man's journey with fluctuating levels of inappropriate anxiety; his battle with obsessive-compulsive disorder (OCD), agoraphobia and panic attacks – having been misdiagnosed with depression and treated with prescription drugs, alternative medicine and psychotherapy – and his ultimate total recovery at his own hands.

How Charles Linden overcame a high-anxiety disorder now inspires and influences people around the globe; and The Linden Method, which he developed to help fellow sufferers, has transformed thousands of lives. Charles' insight into the truth about the emotion of fear, and its connection to mental health issues – such as panic disorder, agoraphobia, OCD, Pure O (obsession) and depression – created a ripple in the international mental healthcare community, which has since become a tsunami.

Charles' experiences from his own life, and working with sufferers of high anxiety and stress, is that they tend to be *handled* rather than treated by medics and psychologists; and prescribed drugs and psychotherapy, which often compounds the problem sometimes for decades or even a lifetime. As a result, Charles was the first person to stand up to conventional medical and psychological practice and say, 'Anxiety disorders can be cured without medication or psychotherapy', and why The Linden Method has been instrumental in creating what has been called 'a new branch of psychological practice'.

The Linden Method is time-tested with a near 100 per cent success rate, and Charles Linden is now probably the world's leading anxiety-recovery expert, life coach, trainer and mentor in Europe, the USA and around the world. His client list is a roster of world-class talent, which includes stars of film, TV, sport and business. When top talent needs a quick solution, they call Charles. When big TV, film or music studios need a fixer, they call Charles. When people need to get back on 'top form' they call Charles.

Since 1997 Charles has helped more than 160,000 people with The Linden Method: guiding them through their emotional and physical challenges and out of, often, severe mental illness, preparing them for true greatness and fulfilment. He gets those results because he knows what it means to suffer and to overcome, what he was told was, deep mental health issues.

Anxiety-Free Me is the story of his relentless struggle to break free from high anxiety. Deeply honest, with behind-the-scenes accounts of the life that led him to be what he is now, Charles tells his story and explains the simple but powerful philosophies he used to guide himself to wellness and which he now uses to guide his clients to unparalleled success, health and fulfilment.

The message of *Anxiety-free Me* is clear: no matter what the catalyst, no matter how long you have suffered, no matter whether you have been told you will always be the way you are, Charles and his many thousands of recovered clients are living proof that you too can turn your life around and become focused, anxiety free and happy in every aspect of your life.

Introduction – Why you should read this book

IF YOUR LIFE HAS FEATURED backcombed grandmothers in stiletto heels providing you with sherry and Sobranie Cocktail Cigarettes, aged eight, while watching *Hammer House of Horror* at 2 a.m. on a Saturday morning then you may identify with the kind of environment I called 'normal'. If not, you may think my life experiences are a little eccentric.

I am blessed with a wonderful family, sometimes a little odd and often with moments of conflict, but the individual elements that make it up are some of the greatest people I have met, ever. They were, and some still are, unique. My childhood was somewhat different to my peers, but was theirs 'normal'?

I have no benchmark for 'normal' since we can't calibrate each other's experiences. However, life has since shown me that some people have to tolerate a great deal throughout their lives and others lead charmed existences. Mine was somewhere in the middle ... exactly where I would want it to be.

Like me, you can probably look back through your life and select specific episodes and experiences that underline your fears and phobias. It could be that you have experienced varying levels of anxiety throughout your life with unidentifiable catalysts; or perhaps there are no clear markers, just a general underlying sense of unease, fear or torment.

The, sometimes, indescribable sensations that moved through my small, and later pretty hefty, frame were intense, frightening and confusing, but now I understand that they were harmless. What a waste of time, intellect and opportunities anxiety has caused me ... although it was ultimately worth the loss. I believe by the end of this book, you will agree.

It's all bullshit, the symptoms that is. I know that now and wish I'd known it back then. The sensations we experience at the hands of our emotions are just electrical impulses within our neurology, but we trust them as being the truth and that's where the bullshit comes in: neither their presence nor their intensity have to impact us and allowing it into our lives is the fatal, but mostly unavoidable, mistake we, as humans, make.

You or someone you love may experience bouts of anxiety as the result of experiences that heighten their perception of their reality, mortality or life experience, as they unconsciously embellish, or create, inappropriate thoughts, emotions and sensations. Sometimes this can even manifest as the symptoms of a perceived 'illness', causing sufferers to fear physical illness even when none is present – often referred to as 'psychosomatic conditions'. That's the kind of deceptive 'mind bullshit' I was referring to.

Imagined illness causing symptoms of real illness, and so creating isolation, fear and loss of enjoyment of life ... that's pure, eighteen-carat bullshit and I won't tolerate it, for me, for you or for anyone else.

Life is a journey of perception regulated by our individual physiology, which is formed by the genetic information passed down to us through generations of 'biological bricklaying', which pulls genetic elements from our predecessors to create a living being with a 'genetic memory' stored as instinct.

This instinct is buried deep in the subconscious mind with few visible markers, except the behaviour that results from it. Add experientially created neural pathways (neuroplasticity) of behaviour into the mix and our experiences and genetics can conspire, under certain circumstances, to play destructive tricks with our minds.

It would be unwise to believe that behaviour is born solely of our environment and that 'we are what we eat', so to speak. This would imply that simply by changing aspects of our life experiences and manipulating our environments, eventually, our behaviour and instincts will change; this is idealistic, but attainable, to some extent.

From the moment of our birth everything we perceive, through our senses, about the world around us is stored and perpetuated as neural pathways of learning. We are born in, what is called, a 'hypnogogic state' – which means that anything that our senses register is handled as 'truth' by the brain. These become a person's core beliefs about life. The brain's ability to do this slows down at around seven years of age. Therefore, children are biologically programmed to be impressionable and trusting. A child born to an alcoholic parent who spends much of their time in drinking establishments would therefore be predisposed to developing a similar habit. However, this does not necessarily mean that all children of alcoholics will become alcoholics. We still have conscious control over our behaviours, even though conditioning may battle against us.

The new science concerning the human connectome – which is the totality of the brain's neural pathways (in other words what makes us 'us') – shows that genetic factors plus environmental experiences equals me (or you).

I believe that everything we ingest, be it substances or data, have to be dealt with by the body and mind; utilised, stored or excreted in some form or another. The connectome shows us that just as food provides the building blocks to sustain life so the connectome is the result of our genetic pre-sets *plus* the use, storage and excretion of data we ingest.

It is noteworthy that children separated from their natural parents at birth and brought up by, for example, adoptive parents, often develop habits and behaviours that mirror their biological parents, despite a complete lack of contact with them. Given these behaviours must have been communicated genetically, and not as a result of exposure to the parent, this suggests that there seems to be a form of biological, behavioural memory present in all humans.

The new science of epigenetics demonstrates that generationally recognisable core changes can occur in the physically and neurologically inherited traits passed down by parents to their children due to external influences experienced during their own lifetime. In other words, expedited neurological and physical evolution. The implications of this research means that what we experience prior to creating offspring may be passed down to our children.

Rather like drugs such as thalidomide, which caused birth defects in children born of the mothers who took the drug, external influences can affect the development of the developing foetus. Professor Percy Seymour of Bristol University once told me how the developing embryo is neurologically affected by solar radiation, (in fact, at the time, he was providing a scientific explanation of how astrology might work). If this is true, then it is not difficult to see how factors nearer to Earth can be passed from the parents directly to their child.

Does this mean that the experiences and behaviours of our ancestors can be genetically passed down? If so, how this 'genetic memory' is stored, or accessed, is unknown, but the evidence is very strong indeed for a mechanism like this being present in all of us. I believe it's present, at least until the notion is disproven, which I don't believe will ever happen.

You may be able to identify the person, or people, within your environment that may have contributed to the development of your inappropriate anxiety. Unfortunately not wishing to adopt or even attempting to block the adoption of another person's behaviour is not enough to prevent it from happening.

You can fight it, avoid it and even ridicule it but, given the correct circumstances, a predisposition to the development of anxiety and exposure to anxious behaviour or anxiety-provoking stimuli, anyone can develop an anxiety disorder regardless of how strong, resilient and immune they believe they are.

Alternatively, it may be that no one in your immediate family presents with anxious behaviour. It may be that the combination of circumstances required for you or another family member's genetic predisposition to anxiety to come into play has never arisen. This doesn't make you immune but simply means that both you and the other person are oblivious to the underlying threat.

Not everyone is vulnerable to the development of an anxiety condition. The mechanism that creates, stores, perpetuates and regulates our anxiety levels is vulnerable to change; change caused by both anxiety-provoking stimuli – such as life events, bereavement, stress, etc. – and the modification of behaviours that 'program' it.

This mechanism is finely balanced in most people – calibrated at a predetermined level at birth, which could be higher or lower than the next person's.

So, what predisposes someone to developing a high-anxiety condition such as anxiety, panic attacks, agoraphobia, OCD, PTSD (post-traumatic stress disorder) and all the symptoms that wreck lives? I'll answer this question later in this book but for now let's just say that it definitely isn't a weakness.

The range of 'normal' anxiety 'pre-sets' in humans is wide, some tolerating extreme levels of stress and anxiety; or actively pursuing it with high-adrenaline sports such as skydiving or base-jumping for example. Others may feel anxious most of the time but because they don't have an internal mechanism or benchmark by which to compare their anxiety levels to the next person's, they are blissfully unaware that they 'worry more' until their anxiety becomes inappropriate for them and an anxiety disorder develops.

When I say that anxiety levels are finely balanced, I mean that anxiety levels increase and decrease appropriately when required. As a defence mechanism, our anxiety fluctuates in direct proportion to the threat present and returns to our genetically predetermined 'benchmark' level, even when this level is higher or lower than the biological average.

So what can we do to change this? Can we modify our benchmark anxiety level? Can we become inappropriate-anxiety free? Or are we condemned to a life of fear and symptoms?

This book is dedicated to all those people who, like me, have experienced the uncontrollable anxiety that undermines our perceived sanity, changes our behaviour and disrupts our routines, our relationships, our careers and our sense of fulfilment.

Myself and the tens of thousands of people around the world who have benefited from my findings, my experiences, and those of my clients and team, are testament to the fact that regardless of what conventional medicine says, there is a solution, a total cure and a 'roadmap to wellness' for all to follow.

In this book I will attempt to present an accurate account of my journey, my realisations and my recovery. To those who find themselves, like me at the end of their journey, hopefully you will find parallels with your own journey to wellness. For those who have not yet started that journey ... it starts right here. For those who are on the road already, I hope you find inspiration and comfort in my experiences.

There is only one reason for the development of high-anxiety conditions in humans and there is only one solution – this doesn't lie in external influences, treatments or techniques, it lies in the simple workings of human emotions and in your intellect.

Perception is a group of nerve impulses; truth is all that matters.

So what is a high-anxiety condition?

In the following pages, you will possibly learn more about me than most of my friends know. My story is one of a relatively simple life marred by a high-level anxiety disorder but enriched by unique experiences and people.

Medics and psychologists often ask me, what qualifies you to help people with anxiety disorder, and my answer is as follows:

• Twenty-seven years of suffering from generalised anxiety, panic attacks, agoraphobia, OCD, Pure O, PTSD, derealisation and depersonalisation; and experiencing myriad physical sensations: pain, psychological issues, confusion, frustration and desperation.

- Creating my own total and permanent program, called The Linden Method, for total and permanent recovery, after I freed myself from high anxiety within days.

- Running the world's largest anxiety-disorder organisation, which has a team of qualified anxiety-recovery specialist who truly change lives; and more websites, media, materials, videos, CDs, apps and books than any other anxiety-focused organisation in the world.

- Helping more than 160,000 people to-date to recover using The Linden Method programs, retreats and workshops since 1997; and millions more via the Internet, books, videos and apps.

- Personally assisting clients, including high-profile celebrities and many young people to recover fully in every case, without exception or compromise.

- Being a spokesperson on the subject in magazines, newspapers, TV, the Internet and appearing on TV shows, including my own.

- Receiving endorsements and referrals from doctors, academics, doctors of psychology, psychologists, psychotherapists, clients, celebrities, the aristocracy and more.

- Developing the only Anxiety Recovery Coaching practitioner qualification

- Producing a demonstrable, near 100 per cent cure rate in our clients, evident in our 2014 trial data.

Shall I go on?

So when a cocksure, shiny faced whippersnapper comes up to me, fresh out of university with the glint of 'newly qualified' in their eye, brimming with academic qualifications and the silver tongue of an ill-prepared psycho-professional poised ready to bamboozle me with psychobabble, parrot-perfect repetition of key textbook phases, like *Karate Kid's* crane stance, cocked ready to fire ... I smile sweetly and leave them a few moments later, deflated and beaten by my deepest of deep understanding of the true nature of suffering an anxiety-related disorder and the resultant true knowledge that I have gathered.

OK, I concede, I don't have formal psychological qualifications. I don't have 'subject appropriate' letters after my name or a weekend course certificate in

CBT (cognitive behavioural therapy on my wall. I didn't spend three years doing a psychology degree or attend medical school … I could have done all those things but I am I glad I didn't).

So what qualifies me to teach people how to be anxiety free? I think the evidence speaks for itself.

What is an anxiety disorder?

The main categories of anxiety 'disorder' are generalised anxiety disorder or GAD, panic disorder, obsessive compulsive disorder or OCD, agoraphobia, Pure O and PTSD.

Why did I highlight the word disorder? It is because none of these conditions are a disorder.

Disorder suggests illness and these conditions aren't illnesses; they are states of high anxiety, which are perhaps better described as high levels of the emotion of fear. If you woke up tomorrow feeling and behaving very happy, would you, or anyone else, consider yourself to be ill? Slightly odd perhaps, but ill? No.

You see, anxiety is the emotion with the strongest outpouring of physical experiences as the body prepares to fight or flee from potential dangers, so every system and sensory organ is affected. This causes the sufferer to experience physical sensations and psychological 'thoughts', which feel uncomfortable and sometimes strange and threatening. In an 'anxiety disorder', which I prefer to call a 'high-anxiety condition', these experiences are constant or come in regular bursts and it is this prolonged state of high anxiety that causes the most unpleasant and lingering symptoms.

Are they harmful?

No.

Are they permanent?

No

Can a high-anxiety condition be cured?

Yes.

Despite what medics and psychologists might tell you to the contrary, these conditions can be 'cured'. Do you note those inverted commas again? Why? Because you can't cure what isn't an illness. I use the word 'cure' because it's familiar but I use it to mean that any high-anxiety condition can be removed by resetting the sufferer's baseline anxiety level back to 'normal' or what I call, their 'birth pre-set anxiety level'.

GAD (generalised anxiety disorder)

Many of those that suffer from a GAD experience a constant sense of unease, tension, shortness of breath, heart palpitations, sweating, stomach complaints and dizziness, for example. GAD often allows the sufferer to continue with normal activities but these become regulated and manipulated by the sufferer's requirements for 'safety', and often result in their perceived decreased ability to carry out career, social and family duties.

GAD can be very far reaching but sufferers may never experience directly associated panic attacks, obsessions or phobias. GAD can be so mild that a person may suffer for many years or even a lifetime without ever realising they have an anxiety disorder or, indeed, ever seeking help.

Many GAD sufferers may be underachievers or appear subdued, shy or nervous but many continue through life only mildly hindered by the perceived frailties this level of anxiety might produce. Sufferers may avoid travel, what they perceive to be, 'risky' business or career choices; they may stay close to home, never marry or have children; or may do all of those things with an underlying sense of unease.

GAD sufferers can feel unfulfilled, in life, in work and intellectually.

Panic disorder

Many of our clients suffer from panic disorder characterised by panic attacks, which can come day or night and wake a sufferer from sleep with a jolt or come out of nowhere, no matter where the sufferer is or what they are doing. Sometimes the panic attack is due to a conscious catalyst, which could be anything from a breeze across their face, a comment or dental examination to a catastrophic life experience. Regardless of the catalyst and symptoms, panic attacks are harmless but frightening, transient and curable.

Panic disorder sufferers often become introverted. As panic presents as the 'risk' itself, panic sufferers 'hedgehog' – which is how I describe the physical and emotional withdrawal sufferers go through in order to protect their soft and vulnerable underbellies.

Panic attacks are overwhelming, frightening and disturbing, often leading the sufferer and people around them to believe that they are experiencing a 'cardiac event'. The symptoms often mimic those of such events including chest pain, shortness of breath, sweating and nausea. Despite the similar symptomology, panic attacks and cardiac illnesses are entirely unrelated in any way.

I had eight to ten panic attacks a day for months towards the end of my anxiety disorder years. I sympathise with all sufferers but I also say strongly … don't despair, as they are curable and very quickly too.

OCD (obsessive-compulsive disorder)

Those with OCD use coping mechanisms to avoid elevated anxiety. Many OCD sufferers obsess about cleanliness, tidiness, danger or health issues; and use 'compulsions' or physical actions taken as a result of their obsession, to prevent or mitigate their anxiety. Commonly, OCD sufferers will, wash their hands repeatedly, check switches, locks or door handles, tidy their homes or hoard objects. OCD is generally regarded as socially unacceptable and sufferers often hide their behaviours from others or become reclusive. OCD is a symptom of high anxiety and not a standalone condition, and can be cured completely by eliminating the core anxiety that causes and perpetuates it.

The anxious 'risk assessments' carried out during flight or fight are the core cause of these inappropriate thoughts and these can focus on, literally, any subject matter. Whether it be health, distance from a person or place of safety, contamination, tidiness, hoarding or anything else that is irrelevant; the anxious focus of any anxiety disorder is a risk assessment and the subject matter is as variable as the experiences, lives, and backgrounds of those people who suffer.

Pure O

Pure O is a feature of high anxiety in which the sufferer experiences, what they would describe as, inappropriate thoughts. These usually have aggressive, sexual, perverted, paedophilia, incestuous or religious focus; and sufferers often find themselves thinking, what they believe to be, inappropriate thoughts about others, even their loved ones. Often Pure O sufferers believe themselves to be evil or mentally ill, but they, most definitely, are not. This will be explained later in the book.

Agoraphobia

Agoraphobia is a high-anxiety condition, which is born solely from a sufferer's urge to protect themselves during the flight-or-fight response. Like OCD, agoraphobia is an obsessive behaviour of self-preservation. Safety seeking is a key feature of high-anxiety conditions and sufferers will often find any loophole, excuse or diversion in order to avoid facing a potential threat. When that threat becomes the high anxiety itself and its avoidance means 'staying at home', that's what sufferers do. Agoraphobics can become reclusive, others move around but mostly with a companion, others can only travel short distances or to places and with people they know. While illogical and inappropriate, to the sufferer it feels very real and very threatening.

Agoraphobia is another example of this 'mind BS' I spoke of earlier. Agoraphobia is not a true phobia, despite it producing an anxiety response when the sufferer confronts travelling or being alone, as there is no specific 'risk' as their location is inevitable – we all have to be 'somewhere'... does it matter where that is if no true risk is apparent?

Derealisation and depersonalisation

Derealisation and depersonalisation are often, wrongly believed to be separate disorders. They are not. Derealisation is the sufferer's sense that they are living in a dream state, perceiving the world through tinted glasses or a misted screen. Sufferers often say they feel removed from reality as if they are a character in a movie of their own life.

Depersonalisation gives sufferer the distinct feeling that while they may know their name, they are removed from that person. When I suffered with this, I would stand at the bathroom basin, holding onto it, leaning into the mirror and although I knew my name and all my personal details, I didn't feel attached to the person in the reflection.

Are these separate disorders or signs of a mental illness? No, not at all. These are the result of the chemical alterations made in the subconscious mind by the anxiety response as the mind and body prepare to take action during the flight-or-fight response.

PTSD (post-traumatic stress disorder)

Post-traumatic stress is the anxiety disorder that most commonly develops after the sudden exposure to an anxiety-provoking catalyst, which involves trauma, loss or injury. PTSD can develop after a simple experience, such as a car backfiring or a difficult childbirth, to being in a war zone. I have helped children with PTSD due to a firework going off unexpectedly and war veterans who were exposed to traumatic events, death and (believe me) worse.

PTSD often presents with chronic anxiety, anxious visions, nightmares, night-frights and panic attacks. Many sufferers, especially adults involved in life-threatening events, use drugs and alcohol to self-medicate. PTSD is curable, despite medics and psychologists often stating that it is not. PTSD is a high-anxiety condition and recovery from it is achieved in the same way as any other of the manifestations of too much of the emotion of fear.

Overcoming a high-anxiety condition

Anxiety conditions can affect every square millimetre of the sufferer's body and cause myriad anxious thoughts and psychological symptoms. Because the conditions can make the sufferer feel unwell and the very nature of the anxiety-response mechanism, sufferers are often reluctant to accept the diagnosis of their condition, often asking 'What if the diagnosis is wrong and the doctor is missing something?'

Diagnosis of high-anxiety conditions is very accurate. The cluster of features of high anxiety is very specific to the conditions and diagnosis is rarely wrong. In fact, in my experience, it's never been wrong. While many doctors are great diagnosticians due to their, perhaps, parrot-fashion understanding from medical books, this same experience and training doesn't very often produce the ability to advise and cure sufferers. Medication is NOT the answer and CBT is inappropriate, counter-productive and often damaging. I'll explain in more detail later in the book.

It doesn't matter how your anxiety manifests, how long you have suffered, how severe your anxiety seems to be or any other measure of your suffering ... you can be cured. I have never in my career found a case that couldn't be. Although I have known some people that have refused to be cured, but this is usually due to their reluctance, for whatever reason, to expose themselves to the responsibilities or activities that a cure would mean. I have also found others who were too lazy or sceptical to move forward to recovery.

I don't want you to think that this book is one man's story and my isolated experiences MIGHT help you. This book chronicles my life, my recovery and the subsequent recovery of every person who has followed The Linden Method correctly.

All humans have an anxiety off switch and I have discovered how to access that switch quickly and manipulate those systems that instruct that switch in order to turn it OFF without exception.

This solution is THE solution.

Don't think that there is another. Don't believe that medication or CBT, talking therapy, hypnosis, tapping or any other therapy will, given time, cure you. Don't think that if you research hard enough, wait long enough or try everything, eventually you'll hit on a solution. This is not a case of 'throw enough shit at the wall and some might stick'. There is a solution, one solution. The solution is psychologically and scientifically proven and if you are human and anxious, it can't fail.

Charles Linden

CHAPTER ONE

The Start of All This Madness

4 February 1968 10.45 p.m., Worcestershire, England

THERE I WAS, born screaming and kicking into the world, right on time, bluer than a baboon's nose and a healthy 7lbs 11oz. Mum was twenty-one, Dad nearly twenty-two, unmarried, penniless, living with mum's parents and, I believe, totally oblivious to the complexities of life.

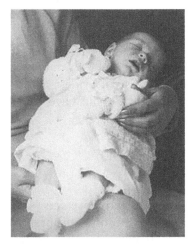

Cradled in my mother's arms. I started out with no hair and have ended up with no hair!

These were the 1960s, post-war freedom gone mad: the birth of a generation of semi-disrespectful humans, fun was there for the taking with very little regard for the consequences. Party beer kegs were all the rage, as were sideburns, miniskirts and the worst-designed vehicles ever to grace the roads, Dad's diarrhoea-coloured Ford Cortina was a case in point; brown vinyl roof ... nice!

Things were very different back then.

There was work for everyone, university entry required exceptional ability, crime was mostly, truly, petty (at least where we lived) and the most abhorrent music to penetrate parents' eardrums was The Drifters and Neil Diamond.

OK, that last example was a slight exaggeration but even as an infant, *Tie a Yellow Ribbon Round an Old Oak Tree*, when heard for the thirty-seventh time in three hours on one of a very limited number of appalling radio stations, was quite enough.

Coupled with the smell of fish fingers and baked beans, the sound of eight-track tapes and a never-ending stream of visitors in drainpipe trousers and bright mini-dresses with white knee-high boots, my memories of that time could not fit into any other era ... but I wouldn't have missed it for anything.

Even remembering events or seeing photos from those times evokes a sense of wellbeing, belonging and joy in me that I have never experienced about any other time.

Dad's comb-over at the age of twenty-one was a coiffured symbol of a much simpler time in our social history. The complexities of the twenty-first century or 'noughties' as they are now known, were a distant dream, which transpires actually to be a living nightmare in terms of the complexities of modern civilisation, social threats and international terrorism. Not to mention the ever-increasing worry of social drug taking, alcoholism, gang warfare, junk food and halfwit world leaders.

Mum took a break in her nursing training to have me and soon became the doting parent. Dad was ill prepared for the role by his embarrassed parents, Basil and Pauline. His mother, who I came to know as nana P, believed that the presentation of an illegitimate child was second only to shaving your head and tattooing a Swastika on your forehead. The shame was too much to bear and excuses were scattered around the community to camouflage the all too obvious truth.

If it were true that nana P were an appalling parent or grandparent, I would stop there, but despite her strange and, sometimes, warped sense of pride, she was probably the best mother and grandmother my father and I could have asked for; the best mother-in-law she was not, but then nobody's perfect.

My maternal grandparents

Mum was an only child of two older but nonetheless loving and more accepting parents, Jim and Kay (short for Kathleen). Papa Jim's only outburst of aggression came when the butter wouldn't melt on a plate in front of the gas fire to enable smoother application on his doorstep toast.

Me age twenty months in nana Kay and papa Jim's garden.

I can close my eyes now and smell his Brylcreem. I can see him stood at the hall table combing back his hair and putting on his cream leather driving gloves and cap. I can still bring back the sensation of riding in the back of his Morris 1,000 to Bournemouth and stopping in Marlborough to crack open a flask of tea and eat cheese sandwiches. That was 1972 and he has been gone for nearly forty years but his memory is etched into my psyche like chisel marks in stone.

The matriarchal figure of nana Kay was a six-footer, upright, able and domineering, but a sucker for my charms.

Born in 1911 and the second eldest of five children, nana Kay was an ex-county tennis player, a school kitchen manager and the finest friend anyone could wish to have, albeit bitterly biased towards me and not so tolerant of my brother, who did nothing to alienate himself but often faced her wrath. I was lucky enough to remain her friend until I was thirty-seven years old but more about her later.

My mum's parents weren't ashamed by my birth, quite the opposite in fact. Until mum and dad got their 'stuff' sorted they provided mum and I with a home. Nana Kay's dad and brothers were the village policemen; her father also happened to be the local poacher and pub storyteller. He would tell me stories about how the locals would turn up at the police house early in the morning seething at the gall of the heathens who had taken their livestock as they slept. My great-grandfather, a conscientious officer, would take up the case with vim and vigour and join in with the seething group and ultimately mount a manhunt for ... well, himself as it happened. Think this happens now? Probably.

I now have the round, brass box adorned with a brass frog with a green stone back in which my great-grandfather kept the weekly pennies for the coal man. I keep it on top of a cabinet in my bedroom as a constant memory of those all but forgotten memories and people, who once lived lives similar to ours, with all the complexities, frustrations and concerns that we now endure. I believe it is important to perpetuate the memory of those who went before us for our children and future generations to appreciate the frailty and yet vital importance of every new generation and our place in society and human evolution.

One of my great-uncles ended up being Police Chief Inspector, the other Lord Mayor of Worcester; scoundrels rehabilitated and pillars of society. I'm not sure whether they continued poaching, that chapter of the family history was omitted. Marie and Do, nana Kay's two sisters in this good cop–bad cop dynasty, were intelligent, friendly and lacking the drive for greatness.

Great Uncle Fred died in his 1940s following a car crash, Les lived till he was eighty-five years old, Do lived to eighty-six, Bert died in 2008 aged ninety-one, nana Kay died in 2007 aged ninety-four and Marie died in 2010, at her own hand, aged ninety-two. Made of strong stuff these folks, there must have been something good in those hooky pheasants!

I remember the smell of stale beer and cigarettes that permeated our clothes with strange fondness, as we visited great aunty Marie and her husband Doug in their pub The Cock of Tupsley near Hereford. I'd snack on Vimto and Walkers crisps while nana Kay and papa Jim sat in the flat above the pub sipping tea.

Mum and I lived with nana Kay and papa Jim at the start of my life and I remember so many aspects of those years so vividly. To this day, I still miss the house where we lived. I remember the smell of nana Kay's cooking; and playing in the garden while papa Jim tended his amazing vegetables and beautiful plants.

Dorothy, my maternal-birth grandmother

As wonderful as nana Kay and papa Jim were, I am not related to them by blood as they were mum's adoptive parents. They adopted her at a very young age as her birth-mother, a young and single school nurse named Dorothy, had given her up due to pressure from her sister and a very strict Catholic upbringing in Waterford Ireland.

Dorothy and her sister then moved to Oxford and Dorothy ended up in Paris, married to a French bookshop owner. It's a long story but after nana Kay's death, we found Dorothy and I now see her as often as I can. Dorothy is my genetic grandmother, which, if you met us both, would explain a lot. Meeting her explained why I am who I am and also gave me an insight into my genetic roots and that knowledge has enriched my life. Dorothy lives alone in Paris now and suffers with Parkinson's disease. She is ninety years old, although if you met her, you'd never believe it. Her hands are just like my mother's hands and there is no doubt that her sense of design, fashion and love of books was passed down effectively.

Despite the lack of a genetic link to nana Kay, she was my nana. Dorothy is my grandmother, yes, but she could never replace nana Kay in any way. However, I still care deeply for Dorothy and her loneliness haunts me. On a recent visit to Paris she told me how not returning to England after her sister's death had been a big mistake and how she never understood loneliness, as people had described it to her, until the point when she was truly alone. Speaking to her about my overwhelming loneliness when I lived in Germany aged nineteen, we agreed that feeling alone brings the full awareness of your humanity to you . . . I described it as 'cellular awareness', which she acknowledged wholeheartedly.

Despite, and also due to, her current frailty she no longer wishes to uproot herself from her apartment in Paris. I understand that but I also feel saddened by her loneliness and the years she lost not knowing her grandchildren and great-grandchildren fully.

Dorothy had no more children with her husband.

My paternal grandparents

Dad's parents were Basil and nana P (Pauline), who was a generous, proud, stunning-looking and loving woman with white backcombed hair, perfect makeup, stiletto heels and short skirts. Nana P stood four foot eleven inches tall and when she was younger had jet-black hair and an eighteen-inch waist. Nana P was, as my grandfather once told me, Worcestershire's answer to Gina Lollobrigida without the fame and fortune but with an embellished helping of diva and an undying desire to shop.

She would drive my aunty Jan (dad's younger sister) and I to Birmingham where we would spend the day in Rackhams, a large and expensive department store, where we would have brunch, lunch and tea with cakes to refuel during our intense shopping experience. Everyone knew us by name and could see nana's white backcombed hair, impeccable clothes and diamonds coming from a mile away. We had so much fun though. Her naughty sense of humour made us giggle as she imitated the staff with her exacting standards. Aunty Jan tittered away and joined in the mocking. As a child, I thought it was hilarious. The trip always ended in the basement, which was an Aladdin's cave of toys.

Looking back now, I remember the surge of anxiety in me as we drove to Birmingham, nana P without her seatbelt buckled due to her claustrophobia, aunty Jan popping the occasional pill to control her nerves. I never felt comfortable whatever I did but as we drove further from home, and before we arrived in the familiar surroundings of Rackhams, I felt jittery and the 'what if' anxious thoughts kept coming; this happened wherever I was but when I was away from home, it was worse.

Nana P's kindness was only marred by her malice; powered by postnatal depression, panic attacks, anxiety and claustrophobia. She doted on her grandchildren but until I was legitimised by marriage – when I was about three and a half – I, like mum, remained very geographically distant just in case the neighbours asked the wrong questions.

My brother (aged about four months) and me (aged four), and yes I am wearing a tie made of the same fabric as my shirt.

The stilettos were nana P's trademark; she even wore them with her dressing gown at night. Only the family knew it was because she could no longer flatten her feet to walk without them. There her shoes would stand at the side of her bed, black and shiny like glass, ready for the insertion of her deformed feet. Nana P lived a dream life, wearing two- and three-carat diamonds, swooping strings of genuine pearl necklaces, designer clothes and black-patent leather Gucci shoes, but they didn't stop her anxiety.

Before her anxiety disorder developed, she would take regular holidays in Italy, which provoked her abuse of some of the language's finest exclamations like *poo-pimey-dong* when she detected a pungent smell or the occasional *ciao*, as we entered the house. The smell thing was never explained and I am now certain it was a bastardisation of something she had heard a German say while in Italy, but quite what we will never know (and I speak German); still, it was endearing and formed what I later referred to as 'Griffithsisms' (her surname being Griffiths). My family are prone to using these descriptive words or phrases – and often to undermine or belittle others – so also often include generous helping of exaggeration. It is always an assumption that when a member of the family says 'it's only twenty minutes' drive' it is wise to understand the statement in context: first deciding whether the distance estimation is to persuade or dissuade you to make the journey.

The familiar 'they' used to reinforce statements was always a favourite, for example, 'they say that eating tomatoes prevents illness'. Often this was used to underline a spurious fact or instruction in order to provoke a positive response: 'They say that buying expensive shoes enables you to walk more correctly', for example.

Nana P was everyone's best friend but the worst of enemies; you would only cross her once. Her venom was lethal, her aim accurate, her rhetoric structured and the desired result disarming and potentially crippling.

I was in my element when I was with her. If we weren't shopping, I was in the field with my aunt's horses; and, if not there, in the Royal Bath Hotel in Bournemouth or at one of any number of five-star restaurants, which we frequented every weekend. This was their life but I was happy to be part of it and nana P really was an amazing grandmother.

Her sports car was a white Sunbeam Alpine, and it was this vehicle that I fell out of when nana P took a particularly dicey corner at speed. The door latch wasn't closed, I wore no seatbelt and aunty Jan was looking in the opposite direction. Turning swiftly on the junction of the Stourbridge and Hurcott roads in the area known as the Horse Fair, I saw the world flash past me as the asphalt created a tumble-drier effect.

I was shaken but unhurt as a passer-by lifted me up and handed me back to my distressed grandmother who, not having immediately noticed my speedy departure, pulled up some fifty yards up the road. I remember this clearly to this day and I am not sure whether my parents ever found out about this event, it was just one of many strange occurrences.

Could this have been the catalyst for my anxiety? In hindsight, probably not, much worse was to come.

Early life

I spent a lot of time at nana P's house. Papa Basil, or PB as we called him, was there some of the time but often away on business. He was also Worshipful Master at a Masonic Lodge the chairman of The Hospital League of Friends, and worked tirelessly raising many hundreds of thousands of pounds for heart monitors and the like. He had a good heart but that didn't stop nana P from victimising him mercilessly. If ever there were a man who should have had a visible groove in his head from the pressure of his wife's thumb, it was PB. He acted as though he was tolerant, deaf or daft; I was never certain which it was.

I was a shy child, of that everyone was sure. I hid when guests arrived and spoke rarely while in company. I remember feeling that way. I remember how it felt, the sensations, the symptoms, the thoughts. I constantly felt timid and avoided people or group activities. Looking back, I can see why I was described as 'shy'; but I was more than shy, I was pretty scared most of the time.

As a child, I distinctly remember forming inappropriate attachments to inanimate toys, especially my teddy bears and soft toys and the sense of grief I experienced if I lost one would be overwhelming. Why inappropriate attachments? I guess because no one else seemed to experience them and also because of the, sometimes overwhelming, long-lasting, emotional outpourings it provoked if I lost or misplaced one of them.

As a result of my anxiety about losing things I'd become attached to, I became a hoarder, collecting everything that had a modicum of value to me, and anything being moved, damage or lost from its place caused me immense sadness and anxiety. However, I never told anyone how I felt, that is unless I needed an adult to help me find something.

I see now that my obsessive behaviour was fuelled by fear, and it is a feature of a high-anxiety condition. At the time, however, I thought my leaf collection, for example, was entirely normal, despite the overwhelming sadness I felt when one of them became damaged.

Things of value

I describe this response as 'cellular' because it is almost as if the mind and body conspire to communicate a sense of deep loss, combined with a sense of loneliness, through every cell of the body. It's hard to describe, but the sensation I experience during this emotion is almost one of self-embarrassment as I regress into what I call 'victim mode'.

Despite this, I believe that the things we possess and claim throughout life are of psychological value, regardless of their intrinsic worth or the value others place on them – hence, the concept of sentimental value. This feeling, which has haunted me since birth, is more than that and I could cry now when I think of those things I have lost … a painted stone, a toy or even a bed or poster from my room. Somehow they all form the fabric of my being and the concept that they may no longer exist in that form is a philosophical conundrum that I will never resolve.

The years I lived with anxiety programmed me to be more finely calibrated to environmental and emotional change. I seem to 'sense' what others miss and perceive danger, atmospheres and emotions more than others; and the formation of deep relationships with everything I encounter is, I believe, the physical manifestation of that neurological reality. Many of the people I have helped also experience similar responses. It does follow that ex-sufferers have an enhanced or even extra-sensory ability that non-sufferers neither need nor have.

Mum and I (aged eleven) in Mallorca. This was around the time I became school phobic. Again, I was never very smiley – deep inside of me the fear was overwhelming but I maintained outward calm. In truth, I knew that no one could help me but also believed that they wouldn't want to.

We all develop as a result of our life experiences and surround ourselves with objects and possessions that define us as individuals, even when those things are not chosen by us. Without these things we 'just exist', or so I believe. If we welcome an object or person into our environment, or accept and tolerate such things, they become, by default, part of our experience of the world, which can never be removed from the process that forms us and makes us 'who we are'.

These objects, by virtue of the fact that we have to walk around them, look at them or interact with them in some other way are responsible for physiological changes in us and behaviours that could affect so many aspects of our lives, without those changes even having to be conscious or on going.

These things can be inanimate or alive, but they must be things that we gather without consideration of their monetary value or, sometimes, even their beauty or usefulness. It's a core belief that there is some invisible chain attaching them to us, forever gaining weight as objects are added to it. Our legs buckling under the weight is irrelevant, what matters is that we don't let go ... or else ...

I still have this requirement to collect certain objects of sentimental value and they travel with me wherever I go. One of those objects, and the dearest to my heart, is my baby photo album. This album contains photos of me from birth to around seven years old. Photos of my brother and family gatherings have found their way into the album towards the end, but primarily it documents the first years of my life.

My son Charlie and I often sit and talk about the photos. He can't believe that I was once small and overwhelmed by how much we look alike; it could almost be the very same person.

You'll find out more about the family conflicts that I still have to endure but one particular fall-out ended up nearly costing me this photo album, so I feel that I should tell you about it now, so that you can see the relevance of it.

My mum asked if she could borrow the album to show a friend how much like I looked like Charlie as a child. Of course I didn't want to lend her the album but, of course, I did.

I'm aware that I neither bought the album nor took all the photos, however, I have kept it safe most of my adult life and it has travelled with me on all of my journeys; it's part of my life. This album represents something very dear to me and no one else has ever really valued it within the family. After all, many family albums have been compiled over the years, but no one ever really looks at them, which is sad.

Some of the photographs were taken with a Box Brownie camera given to me when I was a child. I remember taking the photos and the excitement of having them developed in black and white. The album is also a visual reminder of the start of *my* life. It wasn't created with others in mind. It was created to document my start with photos of me, often with people who died when I was young but always with the people with whom I started my life.

I also understand that my deep connection with the album could perhaps be perceived as inappropriate, from other people's standpoints. However, this connection with inanimate and yet sentimental objects is a deep and permanent element of my psyche born, possibly, of my need to hold those things I love close to me. I could psychoanalyse this forever but ultimately it's my 'thing', to which I have the right, regardless of how people respond to it or perceive it.

However, just two days after lending my mum this precious album one of our regular family fall-outs occurred. I won't bore you with the details but needless to say I didn't get the album back and before long my son Charlie started asking to look at it. Of course, I didn't have it and this was playing on my mind, and now also upsetting Charlie. So I asked my dad's sister for the album back and was told that my parents would 'think about it'. After a while I asked again, but this time received no response, so I asked for legal advice. My solicitor said, that while the album belonged to me legally and morally, he couldn't help me to get it back.

Eventually, after emailing my mother a number of times, I was forwarded some poor quality and distorted photocopies of the pages of the album.

I never thought that anyone in my family would be so unfair, but it just shows that when you expose your weaknesses to people you love, they can hurt you in ways that no one else can. This one incident seems a little trivial now, but as this story grows, you will be able to see its relevance in my life.

I have a deep sense of nostalgia, sentiment and loyalty, which overrides everything else in my life. Family betrayal and sadness just shouldn't happen but I know it does and it has to me.

My grandmother's 'smuggling' knickers and PB

Back in the 1970s, nana P often recounted the story of dad's expensive diver's watch, which she'd bought for him in Italy for his twenty-first birthday present I believe. Nana P, unwilling to pay the import duty on such an expensive watch, decided that the only place the customs officers wouldn't search would be her knickers – and not the one in her suitcase. So, shortly before each checkpoint was reached, nana P would disappear to the ladies loo to execute the careful positioning of one Swiss-made, automatic diver's watch with rotating bezel and luminous hands. It's not known whether nana P wrapped the watch in anything before it was concealed but it wasn't detected and the financial saving was made.

Papa Basil was the spitting image of the actor Lesley Phillips and very like David Niven. Small moustache, swept back, Brylcreemed hair, sports jackets, polished shoes and a cheeky, knowing smile.

PB, as we called him, always had a faint odour of cigar smoke, as he enjoyed just one or two through the day. Nana P encouraged me to take up the habit too, because she enjoyed the smell and believed it to be a 'manly'. PB had a happy face that was, more often than not, unhappy looking.

Just like his famous lookalike, Papa was charming, charismatic and confident, and silently disapproving of his wife's, his eldest daughter's and his grandchildren's behaviour.

Papa often received family invitations to the royal garden parties at Buckingham Palace due to his fundraising efforts and, possibly also, because his two beautiful unmarried daughters, Jan and Jackie, would have made perfect partners for the Queen and Prince Phillip's two eldest sons.

Papa was a much-respected man with strange sandwich-making habits, much akin to the skills of the engineers with whom he worked. He would shape sandwiches with perfect symmetry with fillings positioned in perfect strata of colours of fish paste or pate, cut into perfect triangles with no crusts. I often watched him design and build these monuments of culinary perfection but he never allowed me to sample one. My godfather, Michael, who moved to Perth, Australia when I was two years old, bought a wreath when PB died, it read 'To one of the last of life's true gentlemen', all I have to say to that is no more explanation required.

At home, papa was a kind, loving, generous but downtrodden man who tolerated his wife's obsessive spending and his daughter's Jan eccentricities and anxieties, which eventually landed her up in a local mental hospital.

Despite papa Basil's social standing, it troubles me when I consider how I felt about him back then. I believe my exposure to nana P's blatant disregard of his good soul and efforts conditioned me to feel a total lack of respect for him; to hold him and even, sometimes, bring into play, words and opinions that echoed her feelings. I feel guilt now, whereas at the time, I felt empowered in my naivety of his vulnerability.

Even though I only aired these feelings once, I believe, I hate that I did that to him. The incident happened when he told Miles and I to settle down at bedtime and threatened us by saying, 'I'll box your ears!'

To which I replied, 'You and who's army?'

He retreated timidly and I can still vividly recall the scene ... etched into my memory by guilt and sadness; partly due to my threat and partly due to his cowardly retreat, caused by years of conditioning by nana P. I miss him every day and regret not speaking to him before he died. I have a photo of him on my bedside table.

Nana P's separation anxiety, which probably developed as an offshoot of postnatal depression after the birth of her third child, meant that Jan would wait until she was fifty-three years old to settle down, by which time nana P was too infirm to do her any permanent physical damage! Although nana P did ask my wife, 'Do you have any pebbles instead?' when offered confetti to throw at Jan's wedding.

Until then, Jan had been nana P's support system, caregiver, friend, daughter, punch bag and maid, all in one strong, if highly strung, person. To my knowledge, her strength, tolerance and patience, has only been surpassed by individuals such as Nelson Mandela, and think she should be made ambassador of peace for not having killed nana P with a swift blow with one of her patent stilettos. She'd have got off in court, of that I am certain. The public outcry from local drivers, who feared for their lives when they saw nana P heading their way, would have provided enough support I am sure.

Nana P was unprepared for Jan's wedding because I guess she always believed that Jan would stay with her for her entire life. So perhaps it's unsurprising that nana P did everything she could in order to prevent Jan's wedding to Jim, but to no avail. I watched Jan's health deteriorate as nana P bombarded her with threats, insults and aggression befitting a mafia boss rather than a seventy-five-year-old woman. She was evil to Jan, but her other children tolerated her; they feared her venom so deeply and yet had a powerful respect for her. I'll never understand, however, how people speak ill of people in life and then build them up to be something else when they die.

I think that nana P cutting off PB's privileges would have been futile. For a start, I don't think he'd ever had any under her roof. The way she used to speak to him made my blood turn cold sometimes, such venomous attacks, tuts and undermining comments directed at a man who worked hard till the day he died.

Jan, was then aged around thirty-two and dad's younger sister, Jackie, who was in her mid-twenties, taught Montessori at a local private convent school and when I was older became a valuable source of girlfriends for my school friends and I. Jackie was well travelled, independent and my friend. Being the first grandchild, and her first nephew, I often went to the theatre or to visit friends with Jackie, she was great fun and still is. I attended the nursery school at the convent school from aged four where I once fell over a pal's satchel and cut open my chin. Jackie was taken out of her class and rushed me to hospital where I had five stitches; the scar is still visible.

Did this cause my elevated anxiety? At the time my anxiety was constantly high, in fact, the time I was at this school is also when my OCD started.

Every day I would be sent off to school with my lunchbox containing a bright-orange, glass-lined Thermos flask of soup, crisp breads with fish paste and a piece of fruit, often a banana as I remember it.

Lunch was taken around round tables in a room with a dark wooden parquet floor. On the fated OCD day, I was sat with John, Stuart and a girl, whose name escapes me, when with a flick of my arm I knocked my Thermos onto the floor. Horrified and sad, due to the potential loss of a treasured object, I reached for the Thermos, immediately hearing the *sssshhhhccchhhh* of broken glass as I placed it on the table with tears coming into my eyes. I remember the immediacy of the 'what if' thought: 'what if I swallow the glass', and no sooner had the anxious risk assessment entered my mind had it been etched into my psyche.

It wasn't until twenty-three years later that I completely stopped sieving food and drinks through my teeth in order to search for contaminants. I must have been asked thousands of times why I made such a strange noise whilst drinking. I became ridiculous but only I knew the power of the thoughts behind the actions.

The family pets

Jan ran a dog clipping service from an outbuilding and had a great sense of humour. Her presence came in particularly useful when I turned eight because she smoked Consulate Menthol cigarettes and didn't mind giving me one or two to smoke in the field down the road. When I was eight, Jan was, I believe, thirty-two so she should have really known better. Having said that, nana P would have been in her late fifties and she used to lend me her lovely gold cigarette lighter.

While I was still a baby, there were two further additions to the family: Rusty, a loving but savage-looking German shepherd who, for some reason, formed an inseparable bond with me. As I lay in the garden looking up the sky my view was often momentarily obscured by his enormous face, just before he dropped a canine-drool covered stone by my side – he seemed so keen on the pebble-eating habit that I occasionally joined in with it too. Emma was Rusty's friend, a lovely red dog with a white-tipped tail; also always present as Rusty guarded me.

Rusty's daughter Heidi then her granddaughter Nina carried on the tradition with my brother and cousins over the years; and Bobby and little Hannah completed the canine family. I almost forgot the tortoise Terry, who disappeared under his own volition every autumn and reappeared hungry but refreshed at the start of every summer.

The dogs would carry him around the garden like a giant pork pie, trying – and failing – to break through the crust and savour the tasty filling. I can see Jan and nana P now, chasing the dogs through the shrubs wielding a broom and screaming at them as one of them placed a paw atop his shell and gnawed at it with determination and loud scraping sounds, which made us all grimace. God only knows how that poor thing survived, but he did. Perhaps his diet of dog muck and snails improved his hardy constitution and longevity. I remember being sat at the dinner table watching as everyone around me grimaced, watching Terry enjoy a mound of dog poo on the grass outside the kitchen door. It's funny now but, at the time, it was stomach churning and yet no one ever stopped him.

Life was cool back then. I wasn't anxious. All I did was lie, sleep, eat, shit and giggle. Oh to have those days again.

The first couple of years of my life were simple really and the complexities and frustrations of the family dynamics were unapparent but they were going on in spite of me. Mum and dad married in 1971 when I was about three years old and moved into a Victorian semi in a nice, tree-lined road.

Many awful exchanges happened between mum and nana P, many of which included words of wisdom from my aunty Jan who seemed programmed to reiterate everything nana P's twisted mind could muster. Little did Jan know it, but her mind was being expanded by her mother's anxieties and by these frightening interactions. With each year that passed, she was drip-fed the behaviour, which led to her own dramatic decline in mental health.

My grandmother seemed to hate my mother, well actually it was a kind of love-hate relationship punctuated by outbursts such as, 'Get your bastard away from me' – but then nana P was not really a slave to subtlety!

Miles, my brother

In 1971, when I was three years old, my brother Miles was born. Until that point I had lived with mum, nana Kay and papa Jim. Mum was a trainee nurse, dad had been living with his parents and, I presume, mum and dad had led pretty separate lives. I really don't wish to know the details although mum once told me that another guy had asked her to marry him and wanted to adopt me but, for whatever reason, this didn't happen and shortly later my parents were married.

I was transported from my family home, away from nana Kay and papa Jim, to a big Victorian house where mum and dad prepared for Miles' birth by putting me in a room at the end of, what seemed like, an endless corridor past the family bathroom. There own and Miles' bedroom were at the front of the house.

More about this later but I just want to explain that much of the anxiety I experienced in childhood started at this point and looking back, it makes sense. Taken from what I believed to be my home, moving in with mum and dad, who I had never lived with or spent much time with before, the birth of Miles, the loss of familiarity and perceived safety ... I remember the fear like it was yesterday. Many children may not have reacted in that way but I did.

We all settled into a lifestyle, which was punctuated by mum developing her own anxieties due to the house's overwhelming manifestation of rodents, which would come out of their holes and taunt mum as she cooked in the kitchen. They would sit there looking at her while she screamed before running to the safety of their nests. Dad was working for a civil engineering company and the job came with a comfortable company car, a Ford Capri.

Throughout my younger years, I was perplexed by nana P's insistence that my father had a second family, which she told me he visited every weekend after dropping me to her house on Fridays. Adding my brother to the, already complex, equation was a lot to bear for a small boy like me.

Nana P would tell me in detail of my father's black wife and illegitimate children and aunty Jan would validate the whole scenario with tuts as nana P recounted the tale on the drive back from our weekly shopping trips. Needless to say, my parents were horrified when I told them about it much later on. But by that time I was probably in my early twenties.

It is likely that nana P's imaginative stories coupled with the fact that I was heir to a property fortune compounded my anxiety about the world at large significantly over the years. For my entire childhood I believed that one day I would inherit the skyscraper office building bearing my name that we passed on those highly informative, educational and yet, in hindsight, psychologically disturbing weekly return journeys from shopping with nana P and aunty Jan.

Nana P would say, 'That's your building and one day you will be able to work in it.'

I suppose I really didn't understand the impact of what she was saying but it was, nonetheless, quite anxiety-provoking and I truly believed that my future was a foregone conclusion and that, in some way like royalty, I had be born into a life of structured compliance. I recently told a good friend about this while at a dinner party and her response, without paraphrasing, 'No wonder you were so f**ked up!'

Coming from this particular person, it truly resonated and the reality of the strange, cruelty of this hit home. It's unthinkable that anyone could ever let a small child believe this, let alone reinforce it time and time again as truth in order to secure a firm foundation of mistrust and dislike in my relationship with my father. I grew up believing this fantastic story to be true and when I think of my kids now and muse upon the possibility that their grandparents would do this to them, I can only feel disgust but relief that I was the child that had to tolerate this psychological abuse and that my children don't.

This is the dichotomy I have lived – on the one hand, an ever-generous and fun grandmother, on the other a spinner of damaging yarns.

Post-egg sandwich and orange juice served in a cut-glass beaker among the retail-crazed upper crust, a small child tends to remember and take seriously anything that a responsible adult in her sixties tells them. I believe this had serious consequences on my emotional health and am, in fact, convinced that the continuing exposure to these two women was probably the 'match which lit the touch paper' on the firework of my subconscious.

When I tell people what I was told, I think the disbelief on their faces says it all, as I can almost hear them thinking, *Did he dream this?*

No, I most certainly didn't. None of it; it was all too real for me and all too influential to ignore in this story of my fear. There were many other things I would love to mention, some far worse than these, but I can't. Despite my honest transparency, there are certain things even I can't put into words, nor would I want to.

Sherry and cigarettes

Most Friday nights, aged no more than eight, I was allowed to stay up until about 2 a.m. and at 10 p.m. it was customary for nana P to serve us all a small glass of sherry accompanied by a pink cocktail cigarette. Cocktail cigarettes are safe to smoke because they weren't 'real cigarettes' she used to tell me. I guess she believed that the colour counteracted the nicotine and tar. The sherry I loved it. It made me feel grown up ... and drunk. We would watch Peter Cushing in the *Hammer House of Horror* films and despite being sat on the end of the sofa, cigarette and sherry in hand, looking calm and focused, the sight of a man cooking someone's poodles and serving them up in a pie was a little strong and resulted in me not getting the soundest night's sleep.

Afterwards, I would get into bed in the twin bed opposite Miles and snuggle up on the electric blanket that, after a while, made me feel feverish and ill. Once it was left on after I got into bed, which caused me to hallucinate and almost pass out. Happy memories.

As I discussed earlier, research confirms what I have always very strongly believed: genetics plays a part in how we are, of course, but the creation of neural pathways from data we gather throughout life, form the basis of every decision and action we take. This is now referred to as the 'Connectome'; it is the entirety of our neural pathways, most of which are created, modified and removed as we go through life. These connections make us who we are and if the incoming data is flawed, like a computer, the software stops working effectively: mistakes are made and ultimate breakdown is a distinct possibility.

Our formative years are vital to developing lifelong habits and are ingrained so that they form the foundations on which we lay the building blocks of all that we experience and achieve throughout life. In fact, as discussed earlier, the hypnogogic state creates the basis on which all our beliefs about our environments and ourselves are built. These truths become the foundation for future development and form part of our connectome. Coupled with the genome (our unique genetic makeup) the connectome becomes who we are physically and emotionally. It is, in essence, our very being, our 'spirit'.

I believe that the lies I was told also created in me a need for emotional stability because I remember experiencing a deep sense of insecurity and fear at the time. I often wondered why I never met my black brothers and sisters and why it was more important for my father to be with them at a weekend than with me. Coupled with the separation anxiety I experienced early on in life I believe these experiences certainly laid down the anxious foundations on which my anxiety was built.

This whole exercise in mental destruction of a child was, I am certain now, an extension of nana P's and Jan's dislike of my mother and part of their on-going attempt to undermine her position within the family and my father's decision to be with her. I always remember feeling isolated and different, scrutinised in some way as if my mother and I were a hindrance in some way. I can't exactly say whether this was real or perceived but I know I felt scared.

A skilled sportsman

Dad was a very accomplished rugby player, of international standard according to his school chums whom I met recently at a reunion dinner. I was told, 'Did you know that had your dad not been injured, he would today be known as one of the world's greatest rugby players and that even by today's standards he was a real athlete.'

At just nineteen years old he spiral fractured his leg in six places. PB described the accident by saying that the spectators heard his leg break from the other side of the field, adding, 'It went off like a shot gun ... CRACK!'

After a six-month stay in hospital in traction, his leg was mended but his rugby career was over. He continued to play for the local club from where he would reappear most Sunday evenings, sometimes a little worse for wear and with the odd cut or bruise – which were sometimes from due to the celebrations post-match rather than the game itself.

My grandmother always maintained that dad's hair fell out as a result of the shock of the accident. However, PB and dad always agreed that it was probably as a result of nana P applying neat Dettol to my father's scalp to cure his dandruff. The jury is still out on the actual cause, but my father's hair fell out in chunks soon after his accident and never grew back. I am now partially bald too and so is my brother, so these stories were probably concocted to cover up the follicle challenges that we all have to endure.

On the morning dad came out of hospital, or so I was told, nana P was stood telling a friend about her son's terrible injury and the on-going pain he was enduring. His leg remained plastered from heel to groin. As she finished the story, which had produced the correct reaction in the woman who stood there sucking air between her pursed lips at the thought of such pain and injury, a loud revving sound was heard as my father's Mini Copper S sped around the corner being piloted by whom? My father, gripping the wheel tightly and controlling the pedals with the toes of the foot on his good leg while his other fully plastered leg was mounted through the window, bare toes enjoying a cool breeze. Things, as I said earlier, were very different back then.

This Mini Cooper was later sold to raise funds for married life. As a side issue with regards to the Mini Cooper, dad later told me of how it went into the garage to have some new tyres but was stolen overnight. Dad was phoned in the early hours of the morning by the police asking him to collect it from the bottom of the motorway embankment at the Worcester North junction where it had ended up after the thieves abruptly discovered that it's bald tyres were a good reason for it to be in a garage in the first place. On arrival at the scene a pick-up truck was waiting for my father. The driver, the police and my father rolled the car onto the hard shoulder of the motorway and lined it up to be winched onto the trailer at which point, in stepped PC plod to gives my dad a ticket for having bald tires.

OK, perhaps some things haven't changed, the police, even back then, were looking for the easy cop. Of course, the thieves were long gone.

Family dynamics

One incident I remember, which happened when I was about eight or nine years old, was dad appearing back from rugby rather later than usual, accompanied by mum who had to prop him up as he came up the path to nana P's front door.

'Hello Daddy', I said, pleased to see him back looking relatively unscathed.

He replied, while looking quizzically at mum, 'Who's he?'

Perhaps, on that occasion, he was less unscathed than he appeared.

The family dynamics were pretty dire, as I understand it, but remained a secret until I was a little older. Even as a small boy, however, the problems were obvious: nana P's outbursts coupled with fisticuffs between aunty Jan and mum just went to reinforce that something wasn't quite right within the family.

Dad's social skills and charm have driven him all his life and, despite a heart bypass at just forty-three and other health issues, he continued to focus on building the company he created – the company now run by my brother. I was told that he would never have his sons in the business with him but Miles was funded through school and university and is now managing director of the company. But that's a different part of this story and one that is best left alone.

As for my little brother Miles, well what can I say? He was almost completely bald until he was three with protruding ears and liked picking his nose, (rolling the resultant mucus and reinserting it in his nose, in storage, prepared for later additions). He carried a dummy wherever he went until he was past his fifth birthday and was an annoying tease but also incredibly charming, or so I am reliably informed by my mum. He developed his own language, which only I could understand and teased the family's cats and dog into complete submission. He was a pain but I looked out for him and loved him as only a loving brother would. When I was old enough to drive I took him everywhere with me and was later told that he was the 'Bain Bain' of my friends' lives.

When we would go to a sweet shop together, my brother was often asked by the shop assistant, 'Would your sister like some too?' I was quite feminine looking; small features and long hair finished the affect. It offended me but my brother found it hysterical. He has always been very focused on undermining me.

My only revenge was recommending that he wrap his school tie around his head overnight, in an attempt to flatten his ears. The affect inevitably wore off and tempted him into a much deeper pattern of attack.

Over time, his taunts wore thin; not that they didn't hurt me, they did. They just became tiresome and boring. Did this cause my anxiety disorder? It may have been a symptom of those life experiences and family/environmental issues that did, but directly? No, I don't believe so; I just think they made me very sad.

Miles and I are very different indeed. He doesn't understand me and I don't understand him. That's the way it will always be. I am sure if he were to voice his opinion he would reiterate this fact.

Despite wanting desperately to be his friend and loving him, as a brother should, I could never get to grips with what I perceived as a lack of sensitivity and caring. He always seemed to have an agenda and an ability to cut me down with words that he knew would inflict damage at a deep emotional level. I can argue and name-call as well as the next person, but I always rely on what I believe is truth. I like transparency. I hate lying. I hate attacks on integrity and personality. I am not prepared to 'say everything' as there is a line that I would not cross.

He and I have to live separate lives to avoid conflict.

The funny thing about this is that I don't mind it so much as it confuses me. I have always got myself into this thought cycle that starts with a question and, if I can't find an answer, leads me into a vortex of thoughts. It's similar to considering where space ends ... the fact that there seems to be no logical answer that we can articulate is frustrating. That's how I feel when I get into there thought processes; it's as if I know the answer but just can't vocalise it.

CHAPTER TWO

The Old House and My 'Cell'

UNTIL QUITE RECENTLY I still joked with my parents about the bedroom I occupied in our first family home from about 1971.

Being a Victorian semi, the house, like the garden, was very long and narrow: one room and a hallway wide but four rooms deep including the kitchen extension. The front room was more of a junk room with a table in the centre of the room but no chairs, a Victorian fireplace and not much else really.

The table was stacked with the paraphernalia of a young family but what I remember most of all were the remnants of a huge balsa wood airplane that dad and I had begun to build as a hobby together – although, as most men will agree, this was more for him than me, I was just four years old. The plane was carefully fashioned from shaped balsa wood that dad had bent around a steaming kettle, the wings were an intricately constructed collection of hand-cut balsa, strung together with cross members and carefully glued. Across these was stretched translucent tissue paper, painted with size to stretch it tight. The project was abandoned and the wings filled with holes from prying fingers.

The room at the end of the hall

As I started to explain earlier, my room was the smallest of the three bedrooms and was positioned at the end of a long corridor at the back of the house, just past the bathroom. The room was small and dark and hanging in front of the windows was a pair of curtains made by my mum. The curtains had red-coated soldiers with gold braid, bearskin hats and big black boots standing in rows from top to bottom. My son Charlie now has a pillow in his room made from these curtains. Nana Kay kept them for all those years as a reminder of my childhood. Good old nana Kay, that story will live on for many generations I hope, as I teach Charlie and Florence to cherish and respect the past.

Sometimes, when my childhood comes up in conversation, as it invariably does occasionally, mostly due to the interesting and completely unfathomable path my life has taken; my bedroom, or my 'cell', as I like to call it in jest, is mentioned.

Why cell? Well, it was small, dark, as far as it possibly could be from the rest of my family and it made me feel isolated. It was there that I regularly experienced my recurring nightmare in which I was living on a house built on mangle rollers that moved minutely each day, slowly crushing the house as it did so. This dream stayed with me till I was in my teens.

I also use the word 'cell' as a verbal 'emoticon', a catalyst that 'should' provoke, in my family, a sense of sadness or a realisation that it really affected my emotional health back then and continues to have a certain emotional impact, even to this day.

I don't mean that it causes me anxiety but, when I consider its place in my history, it draws my attention to the isolation and a sense of 'not belonging' that I experienced for so long. I didn't want to feel different; I wanted to be 'normal' because being different meant being alone with the thoughts that drove behaviours that weren't 'acceptable' to others, including my family. I always felt criticised and side lined in every aspect of my life. I felt vulnerable and childish and the people around me reinforced my beliefs by teasing, ridiculing and undermining me.

Did this have a bearing on my later anxiety? Maybe ... in fact, yes, probably. It's all part of an all-too-familiar psychological state that has stuck with me for my entire life. Perhaps the separation I felt was the foundation for my later anxiety, or perhaps it simply compounded the separation anxiety I felt when we had lived away from my dad, who knows?

It could be that my underlying high anxiety fuelled my beliefs about that room, rather than the room forming the foundation of the fear that created those beliefs. Either way, it has created enduring memories of fear and isolation and even fuelled the writing of a poem, which I later recorded, added images to and uploaded to YouTube. That video has had hundreds of thousands of views. I hope it inspires people to look past their fear and see their potential, or at least to contact The Linden Method.

My memories of playtime in that old house are mostly sunny. Playing with the girls from next-door, scrumping apples from a neighbour's tree and playing on the 'tree house' – a 7-foot tall wooden platform – which dad made for us out of scrap wood. God only knows how we survived without falling to our deaths or becoming impaled on a six-inch nail, but we did. To this day I remember dad warning us to play safely on the tree house, and recounting the tale of how uncle Don, PB's brother had fallen from a tree and how his fall had only been broken by a nail sticking out of the tree trunk, which stopped his fall by hooking him by the nostril as he plummeted past it. It makes my knees go weak imagining this happening even now.

I have vivid memories of sitting on the toy-box bench seat, which dad built in the bay window of the kitchen, eating cheese and onion sandwiches with ketchup or bowls of cornflakes while David Essex droned from the radio next to the fridge and mum dashed around the kitchen trying desperately to extinguish the charred remains of something she had attempted to throw together for breakfast.

I also remember how the house smelled and what it was like to sit in the garden as the breeze blew through the hedges covered in white, trumpet-like, flowers; strange what you remember when you try.

I have some very precious footage, filmed on Super 8, of being pushed around the garden by uncle Anthony when I was three in the rust, very broken, chassis of the very expensive pram that nana Kay bought for me as a baby.

I look so much like my son; it's quite spooky actually. It's almost as if I have been given a second chance through Charlie. I hope so with all my heart, God knows I will save him from reliving my life if I can. Indeed, I will do what I can to save all children from enduring the fear that ruined the first half of my life so far.

Family visits

Every Sunday, we would head off to nana P's house for lunch where she would prepare the most incredible array of beef, turkey, steak pie and all the trimmings, and served from her wood-affect, heated hostess trolley. With a choice of nine or more vegetables, a variety of homemade sauces and six or eight homemade puddings, it was a feast fit for a king. There we would all sit, joyously overindulging, pretending that the crap never happened and then finishing off with a dose of Basil Brush on the television, tea served in the Limoges tea service and fresh Cunsell cakes.

Sunday mornings were reserved for visiting aunty Elsie, who wasn't actually anyone's aunt, at least not in our family and, to my knowledge, no one else's either. Aunty Elsie had lived alone since my great-grandmother had died, to whom she was a companion after the death of my great-grandfather. Nowadays such a relationship would arouse suspicion, but I've been assured that the relationship was totally platonic.

Aunty Elsie was always old and died when I was about seventeen but she always looked the same. She always wore a colourful pinafore around her waist and wrinkled tights finished off with tartan slippers. Aunty Elsie smelled of scones and tea and her house smelled overwhelmingly of mothballs.

Even so, I enjoyed our visits to her bungalow. Aunty Elsie always met me at the door with a packet of Rolo chocolates while beckoning me through to sit on her pouf. She was almost completely deaf and mum and I would often have to suppress our hysteria, as she would whisper 'secrets' into my father's ear at a deafening volume. I believe she had been a schoolteacher and, in truth, I was scared to death to speak while at her house, she always made me feel like I was meant to sit quietly until addressed directly … I probably wasn't far wrong.

Starting school

During this time, I started at the local convent school kindergarten, which was just across the road from our house and where my aunty Jackie taught. The school was mostly for girls and it was a lovely environment with nuns at the helm.

Dad and his sisters went there too, so our family knew the nuns well and we often used the swimming pool at the weekends. I remember feeling desperately anxious when I tripped over a satchel and split my chin. Auntie Jackie took me home and to hospital because mum and dad were both at work; even recounting this story now brings back the memory of the internal tsunami of fear I felt being injured and away from the familiarity of home or the care of my parents.

What I felt wasn't just fear, so I'll try to describe how it feels. I used to perceive an overwhelming sense mortality and a sense of cellular reality; by that I mean that I felt very connected to my body as if my 'me' had been removed and I was just another set of cells prowling the planet ... it took away part of my personality, only for a short time until my senses brought me back to the world as I knew it, after the extreme fear had subsided.

I've tried so many times to describe this feeling to doctors and psychologists throughout my years with anxiety and no one understood. Now, when my clients describe the same, I sympathise, fully, understand and know what to do about it and they always tell me, 'You are the first person to get it.'

It's so difficult when you feel alone, unique, confused and scared. It's even more difficult when your thoughts don't seem to make sense or when you feel as if you are speaking a foreign language when you attempt to vocalise your thoughts or beliefs.

CHAPTER THREE

The New House

WE STAYED IN THAT OLD VICTORIAN HOUSE until 1973 when we moved to a newly built house on a housing estate on the other side of town.

The house was built on a slope with typical 1970s architectural features and rather resembled a Swiss A-frame villa. When we moved in, our road was almost finished but the rest of the housing estate was still a building site; an accident waiting to happen but an adventure for two small children.

We would hide in storm drains and manholes, jump from scaffolding and climb in and out through half-built houses. I don't know how we were never seriously harmed. We made friends with some other kids in the road and raced Action Man tanks and armoured vehicles down the hill like go-karts. We bled constantly from our knees and elbows and our skinny legs looked more like black pudding due to the blue, brown and green bruises, each at different stages of recovery, which covered them.

The new house was built on three levels on a sloped road and had a long narrow garden that ended at a railway track. This was no ordinary railway track; this was the Severn Valley Steam Railway. We would sit on the back step watching the steam trains go by as our Dalmatian dog chased our beautiful, white pet bunnies and guinea pigs. Once cornered against the railway fence, she tore them limb from limb. Despite my mother's voice hitting supersonic, multiple mortal blows to the skull from a wooden broom and my brother's screams, the bunnies and guinea pigs bit the dust, one after another.

Dad's attempt to construct the bunny equivalent of a high-security penitentiary was in vain, as all but one of the canine cuties became doggy dinner. The one that got away did so by conceiving a cunning plan fit for any World War II escape film and, with speed on her side, whipped across the lawn like greyhound bait. On reaching our impenetrable garden fence, she found the only gap wide enough for her to get through before turning to face our dog who, while travelling at great speed – with ears following in close second – failed to judge the distance between her and the fence. The rabbit stood proudly as our dog buried her face into the netting with her body cascading in behind it. The rabbit watched as she collapsed in a black and white heap, before turning and slowly hopping away.

The next summer we noticed a group of young, white and grey spotted rabbits on the railway track. Were they the half-breed offspring of our escapologist bunny? Possibly!

Vulnerable to attack

I joined the local Cub Scouts and made a few friends, but while my friends played cowboys and lit fires, I made puppets and put on a puppet show, which ended disastrously as I was heckled off by the other kids with words like 'puff' and 'baby'; these same kids trashed my puppets and the theatre that dad and I had built from an old tea chest, laughing as they destroyed it and while I sat crying at the side of the wooden hut.

Two cousins, who I had known pretty much since birth, were the perpetrators and to this day, my judgement of them is marred by this experience. Seeing them brings back the memory of that event like a neon sign above their heads and the words 'jealous, malicious bastard' flashes in glorious pink above their heads as I attempt to be adult, respectful and friendly in conversation.

This short story encapsulates how I lived, or existed. I always felt small, ridiculous and vulnerable. Even though I felt capable, I minimised my achievements consciously in order to prevent others having elevated expectations of me. I didn't want to show any ability because having ability meant having to do or even 'be' more than I felt emotionally capable to deal with. Despite the pain of being ridiculed, it was a far easier option than being asked to do those things that caused me to feel agoraphobic, panicky or vulnerable. Hindsight is a great thing because, had I known back then what I know now, all of this restricted living, pain, torment and fear could have been avoided.

Camping

One summer, the cubs took a two-day camping weekend in a local forest. Aged eight and very reluctant to say the least, I went. I had never slept away from home before and the prospect of being separated from nature and all its dangerous and frightening creatures by a thin sheet of nylon was almost too much to bear. In my mind I could see myself being stabbed or clawed through the canvas as I slept. On the morning that my parents were due to drop me off at the campsite, I felt unwell, really unwell and made my protests and my fear very clearly known to mum. Mum assured me that I was just getting nervous about being away from home and that the headache and sickness would go off over the weekend as the fun of camp rolled out. I was scared, of that there was no doubt, and I still remember the feelings, the churning stomach and racing heart as I left my parents and walked off to meet my friends at the camp.

The campsite was wooded and the shacks, where food was prepared, made of green-painted corrugated steel. To me, it had the air of a place where murder could happen and no one would be there to help. The trees made me feel isolated but deep inside I also knew that I felt ill and that it wasn't anxiety. It felt like I was in a dream, everything was just too threatening.

I remember feeling so sick watching the kids cooking sausages, which were skewered on the dirty sticks they'd found in the undergrowth, on the open fire as they sang *Ging-gang-goolie* and *In the Quartermaster's Store*.

I couldn't eat. Not only did I feel sick but also my OCD meant that the fear of contamination overwhelmed me. What if I ate a toadstool, a puffball or animal faeces?

On day two, after a sleepless night listening to the imaginary hyenas and bobcats clawing at the nylon tent and the scorpions and tarantulas crawling around under the ground sheet, I felt even worse.

The next day, after a couple of hours of crying, probably one of my best performances to date, the scout leader, who had ignored my protests for over twenty-four hours, reached the end of his tether and decided to call my parents. By this time I was covered in a rash and had a temperature of over 100 degrees. Scarlet fever.

I could have died in that hellhole. OK, that's a slight exaggeration but that's how I felt, and I am certain that the experience was the foundation of my deep-rooted hatred of camping and the requirement to sleep in accommodation that doesn't need to be secured with a zip.

Did this cause my anxiety? I think it compounded the problem and put me in touch with agoraphobia because from then on, I felt very vulnerable when I was away from people or places that represented perceived safety.

Being the 'sensitive one'

One of our neighbours was a professor of geology at a local university, and he inspired my interest in rocks and fossils. My new passion led me to go on many expeditions across piles of grey stone in the vast building site where we lived. I found thousands of fossils over the months and had a pile of Iron Pyrite or 'Fool's Gold', which I used as currency with the 'not-so-informed' local kids.

While I built crystal radio sets, collected blood samples from my father's pin-holed thumbs to examine through my microscope, collected rocks and fossils, and read my father's encyclopaedias, my brother flirted with the local girls and made bonfires to ride his BMX through or over. Even then, the differences between us were monumentally evident. I see entirely why he found me to be a bit weird.

I was always labelled as 'sensitive' and even to this day, people who have known my family for years call me 'the sensitive one'. In fact, recently, my brother said that my son and I are very alike – 'sensitive'.

I don't mind the label but think it needs to be understood in context because 'sensitivity', as it is commonly called, isn't a sign of weakness. In fact, quite the opposite, it's almost a form of super-humanity also called Emotional Intelligence and recognised widely as an asset and certainly not a defect. Used in a derogatory way, 'sensitive' means that a person has a lower pain or emotional tolerance threshold, which might well be how it seems. However, being 'sensitive' isn't an emotional response – although it can give rise to emotional response – it is actually chemical. It just means that the person's sensory organs and the receptors in the brain, which give rise to how we experience the world, are heightened.

Anxiety-disorder sufferers experience this 'hyper-awareness', in which the sensory organs become primed, constantly in most cases. Some people describe this as a sense of enlightenment, of super-perception or of an ability to read people and situations. It can also manifest as sensory overload. Many sufferers regularly wear sunglasses, are bothered by loud noises or extremes in temperature for example. But this doesn't make them 'weak'. It may not fit in with the mean 'norm' but these people experience benefits such as enhanced intellectual and creative capacity, which often outweigh this perceived weakness.

When an anxiety disorder is cured, these benefits become incredible life tools, as they real their ability to experience a more accurate measure of their environment or situation through their hyper-tuned senses; and to respond appropriately free of an inappropriate emotional outburst.

I wouldn't call myself sensitive; I would call myself sensitised. I often find myself sitting among friends and when a situation arises in which social or personality assessments are made, I am often surprised at the lack of accurate perception of some of the others and also, very often, delighted that people like me get the same results.

School life

In 1973, after kindergarten, Miles and I attended a small Church of England school in the nearby countryside, which most mornings we reached by being dropped at a teacher's house just down the road from where we lived. The school was a nice place to be: the children were happy and fun loving, and the teachers kind and thoughtful. Plus, the school food was good.

The school was in a long thin black-and-white timbered framed building, which smelt of sharpened pencils at one end and boiling cabbage at the other.

I loved that school and have vivid memories of winning the school fête fancy dress competition dressed as Count Dracula and drinking milk from a bottle at break times while musing about Mrs Clisset's toes, which peeped out through the toes of her sandals, none of which had a single toenail.

It was at this school that a friend and I scaled the playground hierarchy by convincing every other member of the school that we had been rebuilt using bionic technology and that, under the right circumstances, but never when others were around, could jump over the school building with one leap and very little effort. This fact was reinforced by the 'chuh-chuh-chuh' noise we made when lifting something heavy and humming the theme tune to *The Six Million Dollar Man* as we ran. We didn't move any faster than the other children but the sound effects seemed to convince them.

After I had been there for about a year, mum was called in to the see the head teacher who had certain suspicions about my intellect. I think mum was worried that I had something wrong with me, but it turned out that I actually had quite a high IQ – man, was she relieved. Quite what we were supposed to do with this knowledge was beyond all of us. I suppose, perhaps, it was meant to be an ambition growth catalyst to rocket my achievements into the stratosphere. Whatever it was, it didn't work.

Our time at the house was good but marred by the death of papa Jim with whom I was very close. Nana Kay was left alone in her house down the road but we spent a lot of time, and I think this helped her to get over the loss. I was very close to nana Kay, somehow she 'got' me or perhaps she was just blind to my eccentricities and didn't understand my anxieties. To me, however, she was always supportive and caring, which was all that mattered.

Often, nana Kay and I would walk from her house to the alleyway up the road, where we would negotiate the overgrowth of stinging nettles to reach the 'old wooden bridge', as we called it. We would walk down the new road, stopping by the concrete fountain for a rest and then continue to town where we would do her shopping, have an ice lolly, which I could only eat in public while seated and then walk home. The whole trip was only probably 3 miles but I was only eight years old and to me they were expeditions.

I always felt safe with nana Kay and enjoyed our trips. Miles was only four years old at this time so, to my memory, never accompanied us. On the return journey, we would often call in to see Mr and Mrs Edwards who lived two doors away from nana Kay. I grew up surrounded by big dogs but their mad mutt used to scare me to death. When we arrived at their house, Mr Edwards would try to drag it backwards into the kitchen, where it would try to dig its way out again to get to me. By this time, I'd be sweating, my heart racing, and feeling close to tears.

Friends at nana P's house

My friend Neil and his siblings, Andy and Tracey lived opposite nana P's house and while Andy and Tracey were sensible and older, Neil and I would enjoy a cigarette or two, and perhaps a few swigs of his dad's whisky on the bank at the back of his house. Sometimes, as a treat, one of the neighbour's daughters would show us her bum or boobs – what a treat that was for an eight year old boy.

During these peepshows, my heart would race, I would shake inside but somehow I used to find the strength to carry on without saying a word. Everything seemed strangely scary to me, even pleasurable things but it never stopped me from doing some crazy things.

I remember playing on the very steep long bank behind Neil's house. We would sneak through a gap in the fence and play on the bank, which led steeply down to a large pond and spooky swamp with bulrushes and tightly growing trees with above ground roots.

We had so much fun as we made tray 'sleds' and went down to Sandy Bank, as we called it, a bank of sandstone with a covering of loose sand on which we would bobsleigh.

One summer I decided to build a hang glider from lengths of timber, copper nails and sheet polythene. I carefully constructed it as Miles and Neil looked on fascinated by my construction skills and ingenuity and both were clearly convinced my insistence that I would soon be soaring above the houses after my take-off from the bank behind Neil's house.

Once the hang glider was constructed, complete with harness, we carried it through nana P's garage, crossed the road, went down Neil's garden, over the fence and entered the launch site – all of us excited at the prospect of our maiden flight.

Soon I was inserted into the harness, which was made from dog leads and a plank of wood, and there I stood poised for take off. As I started to run down the 2:1 gradient hill, heading towards the lake, I was sure that I felt a moment of weightlessness and shouted, 'I'm flying' because I genuinely thought that I was. The lake loomed closer but my resolve didn't weaken until, reaching the bank of the lake, I realised that despite the build quality the hang glider wasn't going to fly; and I crashed just before reaching the water. Miles and Neil were close behind laughing madly, tears rolling down their faces as they repeated, 'I'm flying' over and over again ... for weeks actually.

My red-haired friend Neil and I had a lot of fun and that bank saw a lot of activity. I remember being bullied once at the corner of the street by a group of local kids who thought it would be funny to punch the longhaired kid that looked like a girl. Little did they know that our secret weapon, Heidi was as loyal as a sheep dog and would do anything to protect me, and the sight of a sixty-year-old woman with back-combed hair, blue eye shadow, pink lipstick, a short skirt and patent stilettos holding back a salivating, snarling German Shepherd, made those kids drop their cigarettes and run. In fact, I have never seen kids move so fast! I was terrified but nana P's one-woman vigilante organisation had the desired effect and they left me alone from that day forward.

Neil died aged seventeen as the result of a lightning bolt hitting the tree under which he, his girlfriend and a group of friends were sheltering in a pub garden. His vibrant hair and cheeky smile will stay with me forever. The lightning blinded Neil's girlfriend, and I occasionally see his brother Andy. They are a lovely family, great people with good hearts and a very sad story.

The new-build

My parents always dreamed of owning a house in the lane that bisected the local golf course and, after papa Jim died, they set about making plans to sell both theirs and nana Kay's house in order to build an annexed house, which would be big enough for all of us. Very soon after, they found a plot of land on that very lane.

Mum's design flare and dad's ingenuity produced an unusual house that would possibly have been more suited to a Swiss mountainside. Built of bricks, it had an angular roof and was clad in pine slats. It had a triangular window and open-plan rooms, a balcony and a granny flat for nana Kay.

We made regular visits to see the house while it was being built, as dad oversaw the construction work at the weekends. Miles and I would climb high on the second tier scaffolding about 18 feet from the ground and jump off the top into piles of builder's sand or gravel. Miles would make bonfires from old crates and cardboard and burn the plastic packaging strips from the corners of packs of bricks and as the molten plastic dripped it made a whizzing firework noise. One day Miles was doing this when a lump of molten plastic was flicked onto his hand where it burnt a hole that can be seen as a bulbous scar on his wrist to this day. But, despite these risky games, I was somehow always brave and never really averse to doing things that would normally raise anxiety levels.

In 1977 the house was complete and a new chapter to our lives began. New house, new surroundings, new neighbours and friends ... perhaps this would change how I felt ... perhaps not.

CHAPTER FOUR

Another New House and a New School

THE MOVE TO OUR NEW HOUSE coincided with my move to a new school aged nine. Dad's business was doing well and with a lack of an acceptable comprehensive school locally, I was enrolled in a private school having satisfied the requirements of the entrance examination.

Actually, it was there that I met and made friends with one of the teacher's sons called Damien, and he was to become my lifelong loyal friend, of whom I think very highly indeed.

That school, well what can I say? I think until I started there, I was of an anxious disposition, a bit girly or wet perhaps. Sure I had played 'mini rugby' and taken a few knocks in the playground but I was one of the 'big boys' but that didn't transfer to this school.

Most of the kids were fine, but there were number of pupils that made me wonder how they'd managed to pass the entrance exam and a number of others who turned up to school looking and smelling as if they were sleeping rough.

On my first day, I remember feeling thrilled with excitement and happiness as I pulled on my new expensive crested blazer but by the end of my first day all that had changed to trepidation and fear.

My first fight

A small boy, in fact the smallest in my year, who resembled an insect as I remember it; a scabby dishevelled little kid, who spoke with a strong Black Country accent through gritted teeth, decided that I would make the perfect victim for his hatred.

I found out later that aged nine, this kid was a local boxing champion; fast, small and skilled at delivering decidedly painful punches; carefully positioned thumps designed to wind you. At first break, post half a pint of milk and a Bourbon biscuit; he decided to vent his hatred on the most feminine, scared and podgy kid in the playground. Me!

He pushed me, punched me and then kicked me until the teacher on duty pulled him off me like a boxing referee pulling the opponents apart. I stood up, teary eyed, totally bemused by what had prompted such aggression only to see him growling threats at me through his teeth.

My heart pounded, I was scared and I wanted to go home to my mum but *this* school didn't stand for wimps, and I was sent to class bloodied and terrified of the next playtime.

My 'what if' thoughts came thick and fast: *What if he hit me? What if I died?* My mind was busy making anxious risk assessments sent out by inappropriate fear built over years of conditioning, all released in panic.

This scenario was repeated many times over the first days, and the boy's anger at me for not retaliating – as I had been instructed by my teachers – seemed to grow exponentially. His hatred and his goal to remove me from the world was mind blowing. My parents did very little. We discussed it, I cried and they advised me to 'keep away from him' but it was impossible. To me he seemed like a predatory monster, no intellect and no concern for or understanding of the emotion of fear.

I couldn't understand why my parents seemed so unwilling to solve this problem for me. I couldn't understand why I couldn't be protected. I was bemused as to why anyone would want to attack me.

After weeks of torture, anxiety and tears, mum eventually took the law into her own hands. She couldn't cope with my tears any longer so there was only one thing for it – make me fight back.

One evening she came to pick me up only to find me again crying and scared from the battles of that day. On reaching the car she took my satchel from me and marched me back across the playground to around 20 feet from where the gremlin stood.

She looked me in the eyes and said, 'You are bigger than him, you are stronger than him and you can hurt him. You can't let him bully you every day. You have to stand up to him. Now, I will stay here and you go over and punch him!'

I was shocked and worried to say the least but felt empowered by the security of her presence within a safe distance, and so I did as instructed. My heart pounded, I started to shake, but this time, it was adrenaline that was about to be 'used up' appropriately as I implemented the flight-or-fight response in the most appropriate way possible.

My God did it feel good. I walked up to the little scab, turned him with his shoulder, squared up to him and *KUPOW!* I whacked him slap bang in the middle of his face, knocking him backwards by at least 3 feet.

He lay still, as his mother – who'd watched the whole affair – ran towards me to continue the fight for him. She didn't get far before my mum stopped her in her tracks and calmly told her that her son was a 'guttersnipe' who deserved to have seven shades of shit knocked out of him for the merciless misery to which he had subjected me for weeks.

This seemed to hit a chord with my opponent's mother who clearly recognised something of her son in my mother's description and calmly picked her son up and inserted him into their car.

Wow, did I feel better. The fog had lifted, the sun was shining and I felt able to return to school without fear of a rematch.

OK, I was right to be confident but oh so wrong to think there wouldn't be a rematch. In fact, in the seven years I was at that school, I had fifty-seven fights with that same boy, who did eventually become a county boxing champion, but there was one opponent he never beat again!

Tough times and teenage years

Very soon after this prize fight, it seemed that the older children began to think that I would be an easy target for their bullying, too. Of course this caused me more concern. They were definitely bigger than me, they were tougher and some of them were scaled-up versions of the small gremlin just as aggressive and well trained too. I had many fights, I was chased many times and the bullying escalated.

Between the ages of twelve and fourteen, I became very self-aware. I don't know whether this was a hormonal thing or just something that emerged as a result of the bullying.

My self-awareness was centred primarily on feelings of fear. In fact, I can't honestly say that I remember a time when I didn't feel scared to some degree or another. My overwhelming fear of the future, more specifically my death, was impossible for me to reconcile emotionally and intellectually; it made as much sense as the infinity of space and the concept of time, which also made my head hurt and my heart sink every time it entered my mind.

One thing became very clear to me during this time and that was that some of the teachers were as bad as the boys. One teacher in particular sticks in my memory and it seemed to be his goal in life to put us children through gruelling sports lessons, pain and more, and he didn't like me one bit.

He played rugby with my father and I have often wondered whether he was jealous of dad's skill on the field and that's why he decided to make me his new sport. Often he would humiliate me by referring to my weight, and liked to call me 'fatty' in front of my friends, push me and shout at me. But his *piece de résistance* was to drop his keys and demand that I pick them up. When I did, he would take a run and kick me with all his might in the backside. On one occasion, he did this so hard that nana P, who was collecting me from school that day, took me directly to hospital where the doctor concluded that he had broken my coccyx. If someone did this to my son today, legal action and dismissal would be the least of their problems.

I would have panic attacks at school, at night in bed; on school outings and wherever I was that took me away from home.

To me it began to feel like a conspiracy, as three new younger teachers seemed keen to join in the sadistic fun too. They were, perhaps, twenty-or-so years old, fresh out of teacher training and full of beans. At the time, I found their aggression and childish hatred truly incomprehensible as they joined in with the hitting, punching, name calling, shouting and general abuse, while their ability to do anything which even marginally resembled teaching was minimal at best. The bullying went on for years and it is this that caused my initial bout of heightened anxiety, my school phobia and my agoraphobia.

Feeling so lost while at school, I often secretly wished that I had never been born – my general feeling of enveloping fear developed and every day became a nightmarish, anxiety-ridden, reality check. I also felt like others wished I had never been born, true or not, I felt like a thorn in the sides of many people; I felt different and dependent.

Phobias and anxieties grow

As the months passed by my phobia of school manifested. I spent hours crying in the school matron's office, I phoned my mum from the pay phone hidden beneath the main staircase in the school hallway and did peculiar things that I now know to be symptoms of OCD. I cried in bed at night and could feel my mood dropping. I had that 'cellular feeling' that made me feel deeply in touch with my humanity, deeply saddened and horrendously alone and isolated.

I started avoiding chemistry lessons for fear of being poisoned by the chemicals. When I did go, I would avoid touching anything at all and sit bolt upright on the stool, afraid to touch the desk or breathe deeply; avoiding contact with anything, even with my jacket sleeves, in case I picked up a chemical that would later touch my lips. Anything that I could smell was a poison to me, so I tried to avoid the gases given off during experiments by asking to be excused to go to the toilet and then stay there with a pretend stomach-ache or run to matron crying. I felt so alone, so desperate and so stupid because no one else responded in this way and I felt so different and horribly vulnerable

I avoided the art block because I thought that the paints and clay had poisons in them. I fantasised about my family dying while I was at school and being left alone with no one to feed me. But worst of all, every swallow I took meant sieving my saliva through my teeth to ensure that I wasn't swallowing anything that could harm me.

I also made humming noises at regular intervals in class, just to be sure that, when I needed to, I still had the ability to talk. I was obsessed with losing this ability. Freud would probably say that I was manifesting the subconscious notion that my voice wasn't being heard, and he would probably have been right. Whatever the catalyst for these behaviours, I was an overweight, scared and lonely child with no one to turn to.

I was obsessed, scared and lonely. No one understood me and I just felt as if I wanted to die but it wasn't until I actually vocalised this wish in the car on the way to school one day that my mum decided that it was worth seeing the doctor just to make sure there was nothing 'really' wrong with me.

Looking back now, I can't believe it took so long for anyone to take action. I was being severely bullied by pupils and teachers; the teachers were humiliating me, especially the head master who called me 'fatty' and 'girl boobs' in front of the other kids. I would phone home at least twice a day, beg mum to keep me off school, spend most days in matron's office crying and my school work was suffering badly.

What did everyone miss?

Getting help, or rather not . . .

On arriving at the doctor's office, mum made me repeat what I had said to her about wishing to die, so he did what many GPs do when confronted with the trivial anxiety of a young boy, he took out his 'script pad' and wrote up a prescription for two months of antidepressants.

What was my saving grace?

I think, after months of taking antidepressants, the turning point came when puberty hit. Suddenly I grew taller; I developed a deep voice, facial hair and similar sprouts from other bodily crevices!

The growth in stature and the constant fights meant that suddenly I was more respected. Even at this age, I was one of the biggest children in school and genetics had dealt me with dad's natural strength, which enabled me to protect myself effectively, even against the older kids. I suddenly became the protector. Whenever there was a schoolyard fight, I would always hear, 'Charlie help' and I would come running, sort out the problem and usually end up dragging a child to the headmaster's office.

My scientific mind says that the hormones helped to settle the anxiety down, but I think, more than that, my ability to kick the living crap out of anyone who bated me and use the accumulated aggression from years of abuse, coupled with enough intellect to verbally maul any person, including those teachers who crossed me, were far more crucial factors. I was at least now able to exert some power over what I did, where I went and any potential threats that I could counter or avoid.

I wish dearly it hadn't been so, but it was and that saved me from myself and those I was, involuntarily, lumbered with at school.

I remember when the games teacher hid my French books during break time, taunted me, dropped me from the school teams in which I should have played and seemed to support other teachers inappropriate behaviour towards me.

One teacher punched me in the mouth as he ran around the 400-meter track on sports day during the 'teacher's race'. He said it was an accident but no one saw it happen and I still carry the chipped tooth as proof today. No one took action, I am not even sure anyone believed me.

The headmaster, Mr Wicken was nicknamed 'Chick', probably more for the fact that he looked like a freshly hatched chicken than for the 'chicken wicken' reference. This man was hideous and to my young mind seemed intent on destroying me. He behaved strangely at best; he would rock from one foot to the other as he talked, stuffing his pipe with tobacco which he would then light and blow over us. He would sometimes play 'pocket snooker' while rocking from foot to foot and his eyelids would flutter, and as he spoke you could hear the change clinking in his pocket.

I saw this man as evil as he would always call me 'fatty' in front of the class and seemed to single me out to poke fun at. He taught us French for a year and always chose me to stand up on a chair and read from the textbook. French was my weakest subject and I found pronunciation difficult, but he seemed to take some sadistic pleasure from seeing me suffer.

Despite being better able to defend myself, I still experienced anxiety and found travelling difficult but I dealt with it and the constantly changing environment at school; and my love of art and sports probably served to divert me away from much of the most unpleasant anxiety symptoms.

One teacher was a massive bullish man with a face like a bulldog. A nasty piece of work, he appeared to have the demeanour of someone who truly had a screw loose.

He once intervened when a kid in my class decided to whip me across the legs in the changing rooms. I had pinned this person against the wall to discover why he had hit me and 'the bulldog' decided to run from the other end of the changing rooms and barge me with full force with his shoulder.

On finding myself on the floor against a locker after this attack, I stood up, unaware of who had attacked me and landed a punch on this teacher's nose, knocking him backwards against the wall.

On realizing whom I had, in fact, hit, I panicked and ran off with him in hot pursuit. He didn't manage to catch me before I made it to the school office, thank God!

Because of my reputation as a bit of a scrapper, the teachers started to avoid me and so did the kids. I didn't scrap for fun ... I did it to survive. As I entered into my teenage years, I played rugby, I became an athletics champion, I rowed competitively and I did karate but there were other issues, things I wish I had known about back then which still haunt me today.

During this time, my home life was OK. I didn't feel under pressure but I always felt different. I always felt like something was missing, a sense of loss, but I was never sure what of.

Attention Deficit Disorder (ADD) and pranks

In adulthood I was diagnosed with ADD. One part of me was bored with the tedium of school and the other just wasn't able to focus, and the mixture of the two was not good. Not surprisingly, I spent many lessons in the hallway having been excluded for my disruptive behaviour.

Some of that behaviour was possibly fuelled by my own personality; some by the stories of my father's apparent bad behaviour while he was at school. My school had previously been the prep school to my father's school, which had closed some years earlier. Some of the teachers had been moved from that school to mine and the association of ex-pupils still very active, so there was a lot of common ground. So as a child, I felt being at that same school was an extension of a family tradition. I liked the fact that there was common ground between dad and me, and it made me feel closer to him.

At first I drew some psychological comfort from this connection but that soon disappeared with the abuse I endured at school.

Dad described how potassium was dropped into a bowl of water under a teacher's chair, blowing a hole through the chair and the teacher's trousers. Also how a bridge was blown up in the village and some ancient stones stood in a Celtic stone circle were dug up and rolled down the hill. How they had sawn the legs of furniture while at house parties, leaving the furniture standing till the owners returned the next day when it would collapse in a heap when they touched it. He also told me that filling the Bunsen burner system with water in the chemistry lab would result in glorious display of watery pyrotechnics, a choreographed dance of water fountains like the ones outside Buckingham Palace.

What dad forgot to mention was that since his watery practical joke was executed in the early 1960s, was that things had changed in the world of gas science and that natural gas, which replaced coal gas, was denser and natural gas, the one that fuels modern homes, didn't therefore require as much pressure to push it through the gas mains pipes. So what did this mean to me?

Well actually about £500, which was the price the school added to the school fees to cover the cost of bleeding the whole gas system of the water that I pumped into it prior to a chemistry lesson.

Did the joke work? Not exactly as I had hoped. When the first Bunsen burner was turned on, it hissed a little, gurgled, farted and then stopped altogether. My red face said it all and the chemistry master marched me to the headmaster's office. Not one of my greatest comedy moments it has to be said!

Dad wasn't particularly impressed with my comedy either, but what could he say? He'd pulled off his attempt in the 1960s but at least I hadn't blown the teacher's arse off with a magnesium bomb under his chair, an attempted murder charge would have been far less comical.

Another of my wonderful school moments was the day I helped to clear up the school grounds after a summer fête. I was sixteen, a year away from being legally allowed to drive a vehicle on a road, but I could already drive, it was just the Highway Code and road etiquette that I had left to learn. Or so I thought, and I suspect my parents were under a similar impression.

Stupidly, they allowed me to drive my mum's four-wheel-drive jeep around the school grounds to collect all the bits and pieces, which had been left after the stalls had been packed away.

The teachers, on the whole, were pretty impressed with my driving skills and when we had finished, they grouped together on the large drive outside the main school building talking to my, and other pupil's parents at the end of an arduous day. I had been down to the bottom field to drop off some wood and was on my way back to the car park where everyone was waiting.

As I swung past everyone in order to reverse into a nearby parking space, the crowd gasped in horror as I swung the jeep backwards directly into my headmaster's brand new Rover four-door saloon. The car was his pride and joy, the car that, he had just finished telling my father, was the best car he had ever had and that he had collected from the dealer in the previous week.

As I almost completely removed the front wing and then to tear the door panels, not from one but both doors, my father apparently went a strange shade of cream and my mother spontaneously burst into tears as the headmaster gasped in shock.

I eventually thought, *That'll teach the ba****rd for calling me fatty!* Although it wasn't my immediate reaction, of course, but rather the benefit of over thirty years of hindsight. My immediate reaction was more, *Shit, I am dead, I will never see daylight again and I will fail all my exams.*

The reality was less dramatic it has to be said. The headmaster was actually unusually calm; perhaps he thought I had done it on purpose as revenge for his abuse or thought, *If this kid is capable of trashing my car in front of all his friends and their families, his teachers and his headmaster, what could the psychopath do to me while I sleep?* Even if this wasn't his thought process exactly, my God it felt good after the storm subsided. I was embarrassed but perfectly satisfied with my afternoon's work.

This little incident cost my father about £750. Not a fortune, but a substantial amount of cash to hand over in 1983.

Through all this turmoil though, my anxiety constantly poked its head up. I never felt comfortable on school trips, school skiing holidays or outings. I didn't like being at school, away from a place of safety or security; it felt foreign, lonely and cold, I was scared but I kept the emotions at bay by keeping busy.

Projects

I was a born dismantler but I had become a builder too. Aged thirteen I built a captain's bed in my bedroom and a desk with a compartment. I built various electrical systems and once wired the house for sound and transmitted music and my voice from the garage.

Pictured on my Yamaha DT125.

As I got older I started tinkering with old motorbikes too, and dad bought us a 100cc-racing go-kart that we would race around the massive car park in the middle of the largest local traffic island. We had so much fun.

Miles and I both had motorbikes. Mine was an ex-road bike that had been converted into a trial's bike, which I stripped down and rebuilt before painting the tank bright red. Miles had a 50cc Honda.

We would ride them up and down the drive at every opportunity and at weekends, we would push them across to Spennels Valley – partly a nature reserve but mostly wasteland, woods, streams and natural sand pits.

Dad would give us our pocket money and, after filling up with petrol at the garage, off we would go aged thirteen and nine. We'd be gone all day. Mum and dad mostly had no idea where we were or what we were doing. We'd race around all day and sometimes the motorcycle police would be dispatched to catch us, but they were no match against our little dirt bikes and we'd always get away. As we got braver, we would pull up and allow the officers to dismount and walk towards us before starting up and riding away. Of course, they'd try to chase us but by the time they had their helmets on, we were gone.

They once stopped us on the main road en route to the garage to fill up with petrol, explaining that it was illegal for an unlicensed, untaxed and uninsured motorcycle to touch the highway, especially under the care of a minor.

We pushed the bikes home where we taped up the brake lever and peddle and strapped our old roller skates to our wheels. When the police stopped us on the way home a few weeks later, there was nothing they could do as we explained that the skates acted as a 'trailer' and the wheels weren't touching the highway.

I admit these encounters filled me with anxiety fuelled by the fear of authority instilled into me by school and our parents, and on one occasion, as we were being pursued by the police through the woods and the police bike was gaining on us, I did become very breathless and thought I was having a heart attack. On that occasion I rode the bike all the way home along the road. It was a panic attack of course.

More dangerous exploits

My friend Nick, who was made of steel, and I went over to Spennels Valley to play on the rope swing which was aptly named 'the killer' by the local kids. The rope extended over 30 feet above a bank and at the bottom of the bank was a wide stream. In our infinite wisdom, we thought it would be fun to fetch bales of hay from the unattended barn on the south boundary of the valley and create a makeshift safety net onto which we could dive as the swing reached its furthest point just across the stream.

We carefully executed the jumps, landing in the thick hay. It was Nick's turn and we were getting cocky. As he released the rope, I could see that he had misjudged and I felt that familiar pang of fear as my chest jolted with a shot of adrenaline.

Nick hit the floor shoulder first and bounced as I watched in horror. He rolled around in obvious agony, grasping his arm and crying out. I ran down the bank as fast as I could. By this time my heart felt like it would break out of my chest as my thoughts cycled fast with 'what if's'.

Nick's forearm had an extra bend below the elbow and was so badly broken that it turned at almost ninety degrees. I could feel the panic building but we were two thirteen-year-olds, 2 miles from home and I knew that we needed to get him to hospital.

Mobile phones were a few years off yet so I did what we had to do. I put mine and Nick's BMX bikes on my shoulders, made my T-shirt into a sling and placed Nick's arm carefully in it, and walked slowly home to our house where my brother and another friend, Malcolm, were playing. Nick's mum was working so my mum raced us to hospital.

We waited for over two hours to be seen and just as Nick was called in, the A&E doors opened and in walked Malcolm clutching his arm. He then said 'I went over Spennels to see how Nick had broken his arm and I let go too soon.'

Malcolm had the exact same break: same arm, same shape. It was beyond belief. For weeks, Malcolm and Nick walked around, each with their same arm in plaster. Looking back it was comedic but at the time it escalated my anxiety. The adrenaline had been used appropriately during the period in which I needed to take action but it continued long after, spinning away within me as I relived the accident in my head again and again.

Shortly after this happened one of my school friends was killed in a road accident as he rode his bike home from a friend's house. The grief and solemn atmosphere at school compounded my anxious thought patterns and my I could feel my heart racing as I my mind whirled round in a constant cycle of morbid thoughts. No one cared.

Miles (aged nine) and me (aged thirteen) in school uniform. Pictured with us, our dog Ollie, who would fart when he barked, which used to embarrass us all when we had guests over. He was a lovely dog though, despite his lack of etiquette.

Although safe from, what the school would tell you, are the more threatening or negative elements of society, this school cocooned its pupils in what masqueraded as safety. The school was actually a closed shop. The teachers, on the whole, supported each other in their cruel games and protected each other from potential scrutiny. The problems stayed local, they were suppressed, hidden and overlooked. The environment was controlled and secret, oppressive and frightening.

I remember these teachers being bullies. They would name-call, smack and punish us more than the other teachers. One would watch us in the showers and make inappropriate remarks. He would also slipper us on our bare backsides.

Perhaps these people wouldn't have the same opportunities if they'd been working in a state school where classes are larger and teachers are correctly qualified, guided and screened. The mental torment I endured at this school seems small fry against the monumental hideousness of such crimes and illnesses but to a young lad with anxiety problems, most of my challenges seemed as monumental.

I punched and kicked my way through school with few real friends and, as I started to mature, I began to realise that my peers were, on the whole, selfish and ignorant to what I was going through; at their age, why should they care if I suffered each and every day.

It seemed too that the other children were, on the whole, spoiled with gifts and holidays, which served to alienate me further yet from 'the pack'. When video recorders were launched, it was nearly two years before we had one at home and then dad, in his infinite technical wisdom, decided to buy a Phillips 2000 VCR, for which the local video shop had no hire tapes.

My friends would boast about having watched the latest movie or having accidentally happened across a selection of their parents' porn collection on Betamax while I could only record broadcast programmes from the four available TV channels at that time and pretend that I too had watched *Zombies Dawn of The Dead* at the weekend.

The 'carrot-dangling' taunts of the 'rich kids' with the latest technology got me down, alienated me and caused me to feel even less of an 'equal'.

One such child, an obnoxious but quite handsome bighead was a particular bore. On my fifteenth birthday my classmates asked what technological marvel I had received. I had been given a rather handsome if cumbersome cassette radio, of which I was pretty proud, so I commenced to describe it to my friends when this kid interrupted me with, 'Well, mine is far better than ...'

He didn't reach the end of his sentence because of the powerful and well-guided punch, which I carefully administered to his much too-chiselled jaw on his much too smug face. After standing up, his look of total dismay gave him away and my classmates laughed uncontrollably as he sloped off to bathe his bruised ego. He never did it again.

Yes, the burst of adrenaline he caused added to my, already sky high, anxiety and the result was, perhaps, a little harsh in hindsight but when I think back to the enduring fear and pain I felt each day, it wasn't at all surprising.

Growing up and girls

As I approached fifteen, I started to develop a flair for athletics and rugby. I lost weight and became quite fit. I even joined the local rowing team, rugby team and played squash and learned karate. Things slowly started to come together for me and as they did, I discovered something far more interesting... women; and even better, they discovered me!

Until that point I had been the chubby brunt of many a joke but suddenly, I was taller and leaner. The puppy fat breasts had gone and now felt just a tad firmer. Suddenly, with my new body hair and height, I became just that bit more popular than my peers and they hated it; the competition had begun and I had a head start.

They taunted me and bated me about the latest girlfriend, but it was like water off a duck's back. I knew now that their jibes were born of jealousy not superiority and that put me into a position of power, which made a refreshing and very needed change.

I can't say I was anxiety free because the very same fears and phobias, although minimised, were still present. They were a constant reminder of my mortality and the frailty of life, which reared its head mostly when I felt down or tired. The childhood thoughts and fears were still there when I allowed them the mind space to exist.

Each new encounter with the opposite sex brought on new emotions and with the excitement came anxiety and sometimes I found it very difficult to separate the two. I remember girls asking me why I was shaking, as we kissed which wasn't easy, but I always passed it off as excitement, which seemed to placate them. Would the truth have scared them away?

Even my first encounter with a girl was marred with anxiety I can remember my first girlfriend, grabbing me and kissing me passionately, hoping to produce the desired response but all I did was shake. I can still remember it today, I felt like I was plugged into mains electricity, my heart raced and my body quivered like a scared rabbit; how stupid I felt. When she then requested that we move the relationship to a more physical level, which was done through a not so subtle hand gesture, the panic gripped me and I ran.

Academically I seemed to float around in the middle of the top stream and struggled to maintain descent grades in math's and chemistry, which caused the eventual demise of my dream of becoming a surgeon. I hardly ever focused and I was bored at school and spent most break times filling the master's briefcase with grasshoppers and making people laugh.

I spent break times in the woods smoking or kissing one of the dozen girls in our school and the world seemed a bit more interesting, a little less threatening and a good place to be for a while.

My first sexual encounter was at school with a sixteen-year-old girl. One of the older children fetched me from the playground saying that I was needed in the squash court. On entering, the door was locked behind me as this girl dragged me onto the gym mats, undid my trousers and did the, at that time, unthinkable to me.

Half of me thought Christmas had arrived early; the other was too terrified of the unending shame that running from the building screaming would have brought. I shook, I felt breathless, I didn't know what to do and mostly, I couldn't perform as she wished and after she had been satisfied by my attempts, she gave up and kicked me out. I was so relieved as I ran to the senior locker room and had a panic attack.

Despite my evident lack of sexual prowess, I no longer felt threatened as I walked through school, the bullying had stopped long enough ago for my anxious behaviour to subside along with the constant threats and on the whole, my days were fearless.

Occasionally I would feel very anxious. A school skiing trip, for example, made me very anxious for the week I was there. The worst I felt was when a lad in my class stole a huge sample bottle of perfume from a shop in the ski resort and the police travelled from Trento, dozens of miles away, to search the hotel. It was in my room. Nothing to do with me but even so, the thought of being locked up with a gang of Italian criminals and used as their 'bitch' was too much for me. I made the guy who stole the perfume take it back but he didn't. Instead he threw it out of our window into a snowdrift where it wouldn't be found till spring.

I remember being terrified and was so glad to get home.

The deep-rooted anxiety of life, however, was ever present and simmering beneath the surface, and was a constant reminder of how I once was. I had no idea that this low-grade anxiety was also to become the trickling source of a far greater torrent of extreme and acute anxiety; the catalyst and the seed from which would grow the overpowering and intense anxiety disorder, which would be the foundation for a decade of pain, misery and missed opportunities.

I met my first real girlfriend at a tennis club disco. She was actually going out with another kid in my class, the one with the chiselled jaw I nearly broke.

This girl was very pretty and kind and above all, she liked me in a way that no one had ever liked me before. My godfather seemed to like her too, especially when she emerged from his swimming pool in a see-through, yellow swimming costume, her dark brown skin glistening with water, she seemed to appeal to all my dad's friends . . . strange that!

Over time, it turned to love and she promised to be mine forever. Like a fool, I trusted her. Boy did I have a lot to learn.

I was the envy of my friends, the first to have a real girlfriend, the first to have sex. Suddenly I was cool and instead of being alienated as a tubby nerd, I was now alienated as a threat. But this time the whip didn't sting like before because this time I was not the victim. My anxiety simmered below the surface but, ultimately, it was under control and so was my life, it seemed.

Preparation for the future

Leaving that dreadful school was a dream come true. However, I believe that what I learned there prepared me well for helping the many tens of thousands of young people who have recovered as a result of using my programs.

People tell me that the level of understanding I have of their predicament and suffering is so powerful and compelling during their recoveries. I love that. I love helping people.

I know what it is like to be an anxious child. I have had every thought symptom and sensation. I have felt the loneliness, the isolated fear, the torment of the simplest and most innocuous interaction between a teacher and myself. I have been over-tuned to people's moods and the nuances of personalities. I know what it is to have a panic attack because of a bumpy road surface or because someone says 'you look tired', I know what it is like, as an anxiety sufferer, to visit the dentist, go to the doctor or have hospital tests.

Always feeling anxious, no matter how safe you truly are, is tiring, frustrating and more than anything, scary.

As a child, I didn't understand why I was different to other kids. I didn't know what questions to ask or how to describe how I was feeling. In fact, I didn't understand the notion of how I was any different to anyone else so asking about how I felt was never something I felt compelled to respond to.

Now, looking back, I was so, so scared. I was so withdrawn at so many points when I should have been planning and moving forwards. ADD played a part but my anxiety was the real problem and had I known to address it, my life path would have been much different. But I wouldn't change those experiences now, as I love what I do and wouldn't want to erase that opportunity.

I now see why my family thought I was strange, weird, moody and withdrawn. I understand completely that my feeling of isolation was compounded by my inability to cope with the anxiety-fuelled anger I experienced whenever I felt ridiculed, cornered or attacked. I was able to punch my way out of many situations but I wasn't ever really able to control my emotional outbursts, but now I know why.

It's so easy for people to make decisions based on other people's visible responses and to respond according to their own life experiences and the wiring that forms their own personal 'connectome', but when a person with anxiety feels vulnerable, isolated and scared, how else are they to respond?

Self-preservation in anxiety sufferers causes a 'flight or fight' response to withdraw, to fight, to run away; not just from real threats but from responsibility, from adult behaviour, in fact from everything that doesn't belong within the fight or fight mechanism. This explains why anxiety disorder sufferers avoid intimacy, sex, work, reading and hobbies because, while in the flight-or-fight response, the mechanisms and resources to perform those day-to-day tasks and activities are diverted to *fight* threat. For the first twenty-seven years of my life, in fluctuating levels, I was primed to defend myself against threat and many of my other faculties were switched off.

Recently I said to my mum that throughout my life I have had experiences when interacting with other people that have caused me a sense of frustration so strong that I had wanted to run away and hide for the rest of my life. I asked her, 'Have you ever felt, when you try to explain how you are feeling and you are convinced that the situation you are describing or your viewpoint is correct, that you are speaking a foreign language?'

Sometimes I feel that the person with whom I am speaking is either contesting me, in order to frustrate me, or won't admit that they are, perhaps, wrong or don't 'get it'. This is, of course, their failing, not mine, so I no longer allow it to impact on my happiness.

I now see why I felt so isolated as a child. I also see why some people go about life happily without a care. I also see why the world is a better place with anxiety sufferers in it . . . and that when they have recovered, which they always will with the correct guidance, they become amazing resourceful people.

On my last day at that school, I was hailed into the headmaster's study so that he could officially confirm that my fifty-seven fights with the same child were just a fraction of the one-hundred-and-ninety fights I had at that school and to tell me that I would never make anything of my life.

Well headmaster, if you were still alive and hadn't died, allegedly of a sexually transmitted disease, I would tell you of how my life is now and how my experiences at the hands of the student's bullying and his dreadful, abusive headmastering were part of that success.

I would also tell him about how many people, The Linden Method has helped across the world and how many bullied children have benefited from my experiences and advice.

CHAPTER FIVE

Sixth-form Hell

HAVING DONE THE IMPOSSIBLE, passed my exams, I gained a place as a dayboy at sixth form in a prestigious school some 7 miles from home. Securing a place there was mainly due to my ability on the rugby field, (which was improving despite the distraction of my girlfriend) and my talent in art and design, especially drawing, which I loved.

Aged seventeen *with* hair.

I was scared of the change but a number of other children from my school had gained places there.

It was funny but a number of the 'ladies' that lunched', the gaggle of non-stop gossips who collected around the school masters at the end of school, hoping that their flirtatious glances might in some way secure their children's academic success, decided that I must have cheated during my exams and so reported me to the examination board; all because I had gained higher grades than their perfect and 'clearly' academically superior children.

My parents were horrified, but I laughed off their accusations, so while they shipped their children off to re-sit exams I was buying my grey suit and commencing my further education at my school of choice.

Sure I was disruptive to an extent, always the joker, always getting into trouble and chatting when I shouldn't be, but I passed my exams. How could I have done that without knowing the material? Cheating? It's not in me to cheat. I was too scared of being found out and the 'messing around' was a mask I used to hide my fears.

New places and faces

My sixth form school was an ex 'Bluecoat' military boarding school, which was ruled by an extreme headmaster and his henchmen, the boarding house monitors. These chosen few acted like Gestapo officers, only possibly more sadistic, in some cases, sexually deviant and often devoid of any compassion or common sense. The headmaster seemed to have little idea about what went on behind closed doors. Alcohol consumption was allowed for those of legal age with parental consent, as was smoking. However, growing cannabis and smoking it behind the local Chinese restaurant wasn't allowed, even if your parents were raving 'hash head hippies' who were happy for their kids to get stoned between lessons. Sexual deviants, drugs, alcohol, they had them all at that school but it was never made public or addressed officially, it was all cleanly swept under the rug.

This school masqueraded as a centre of excellence, strict, regimented and tidy. It wasn't at all, it was ruled with threats and the teaching staff seemed mostly ineffectual at best.

I hated this school. To me if felt like a home for deviant boys. For example, birthdays were celebrated by dozens of boys chasing the scared youth until he collapsed. The seething morons then carried the poor birthday boy to the boarder's bathrooms to be 'dunked' in a bath of water, dog and human shit, rotten packed lunches, urine and any other foul substance that could be found in or around the school premises.

Having been held under the surface for a prolonged period, the boy was then released, chased again and, when captured, some creep would scream 'pile on', which resulted in the captive being crushed, sometimes to unconsciousness, by the two dozen 'chasers' who found it all so hysterical.

I was pretty big and strong by this time and held the record for surviving through my sixth form years without being dunked. This was probably because I gave my classmates a warning on the morning of my birthday to the effect that I would fight if a dunking were on the cards. Unfortunately, they didn't heed my warning, which resulted in a large and particularly aggressive boy being rushed to the sanatorium with a broken nose but it had the desired effect of putting off the chase.

The following year the warning was surplus to requirements and I enjoyed a reasonably happy birthday without my celebratory bath.

Initially both prefects and teachers pushed me around but I could handle myself by this time and they knew that I wouldn't take the abuse that other kids did. I didn't care about my schoolwork at this point. I was fed up with the nonsense these bullies, kids and teachers fed to us.

It's strange actually that at this time I would feel nervous about going on a coach trip or travelling away from home but I was, controlled and confident when it came to standing up for others and myself. I think the other boys trusted my strong morals and sense of propriety: they knew I only acted when required and otherwise walked away. I now know that this is a feature of people who suffer with anxiety disorder; an undying need to help others coupled with tenacity and integrity.

On a number of occasions, certain boys had been caught doing some pretty nasty things to the younger kids. The 'old school' fagging was rife. (Fagging is when the younger boys are made to do unpleasant tasks for the older boys in the boarding houses; this even included some pretty horrific sexually motivated acts.) It wasn't unusual for a group of young children to find themselves naked doing press-ups or running around the gym. The 'requests' made by some of the boys often left me feeling disgusted and on a couple of occasions forced me to take matters into my own hands by warning off the older kids when I caught them being unreasonable or unpleasant. To my mind, the school was badly run and a damaging place for children.

I became particularly unpopular when a house master, who organised the inter-school rugby tournaments, asked me to play two games over a single weekend when I had planned to go away with my girlfriend. It was a last-minute request and I refused. This sin resulted in me being summoned to the headmaster's office where I was asked to explain myself, which I did. I wasn't asked to leave the school but I thought they would. Instead I was told to turn up for the game the next day, which I did like a good boy. It was the last game I ever played.

Bunking off

My attendance was poor but it didn't matter. I was disinterested at best. I would sign the register at 8.30 a.m., attend assembly and then go to my car, sometimes accompanied by friends, and leave. Sometimes I would take them all shopping or to a park. On one occasion I drove to Birmingham to meet a very pretty girl, Vanessa, who I had met in a nightclub the previous Friday. We met at the train station and walked up to the new shopping centre that had opened that day. On the way through, we were stopped by a journalist asking for the public's views on the modernised centre, which I answered politely and then Vanessa and I posed for a photograph.

Two days later, returning from school, dad asked me how I was enjoying my week and whether I had been 'skiving off' school at all. Scared to death that he'd find out I had been 'skiving' quite a bit recently, I responded in the negative, and tried to put on my most convincing grimace at the thought that I would ever do such a dreadful thing.

At that, dad pulled out a copy of the *Birmingham Post* and there, slap bang centre of page one were Vanessa and I.

I have never lived that one down. In fact, I still have the clipping as a reminder of my deceit! I hate lying but self-preservation is vital!

I made some good friends at school and my anxiety was kept at bay by the constant use of my excess adrenaline by being poised in 'self defence mode' most of the time, looking over my shoulder to be sure that I wasn't going to be lynched by a group of psychotic, 'pool ball in sock' yielding hooligans.

I wasn't immune to their behaviour and once had my study desk shelves tipped on me by one hooligan. I also had people jump me from behind, and it became a pastime for some kids to try to 'get me' if they fancied their chances. It was tiring, intimidating and frightening, and had I been a smaller weaker child, I am sure the damage would have been greater. I have since heard of kids being treated like this who later suffered from mental illness and worse. Why is society so twisted? I have never, ever attacked someone unprovoked. Whatever possesses people to do so?

I had joined the school in an attempt to satisfy my parents' requirement for a certain level of success but it bored me, it didn't create any income and there weren't any girls. I am still not sure what my parents wanted for me ... Happiness? Success? I just knew that I was bored with learning this way and I believed that they just wanted me to smile more and be 'normal'.

New friends and a band

I met some boys who played instruments and we formed a band called 'Kyoto', a direct reference to our joint enjoyment of the band 'Japan', the lead singer of which, I was told, I resembled.

I couldn't really sing well at all but I was the most tuneful of my friends and tried desperately to grapple with the lyrics of the strange songs we composed while being in deep-rooted turmoil about performing in public. I looked the part. Highlighted 1980s style hair, weird 'new-romantic' style clothes and big glasses.

The anxiety took over but I didn't let it beat me.

Even when just a handful of people sat in on rehearsals, I sometimes felt the room spin as my heart felt as if it were about to burst through my chest onto the floor. I knew that my anxiety was much higher than my friends were experiencing but somehow theirs seemed more appropriate and while I knew I was truly suffering, I had no 'benchmark' by which to compare levels.

I have always said that what an anxiety sufferer really needs is to belong to the 'Borg', the race of machine/human hybrids from *Star Trek*. They belonged to a collective, each one existing as separate components of a larger whole; living as one but able to access a group consciousness.

How useful would it be for anxiety sufferers to have the ability to calibrate their minds, to reset faults or psychological issues or even to be able to make comparisons that enable us to receive immediate knowledge, security and peace? If only we could plug into each other in order to understand and compare psychological, social and moral issues from other people's standpoints. Wouldn't that make politics of people and states so much easier to negotiate? Wouldn't the world be a more balanced place? Who knows?

Girls, girls, girls

Throughout school I stayed with the same girl, Erica, and we enjoyed skiing holidays and summer breaks on the coast with a group of her friends, which was an adventure I can tell you – me and five sixteen-year-old convent schoolgirls alone in a cottage in Devon. At first I was scared by the prospect but having half-naked young women around me for a week soon lulled me into a complete sense of contentment. Nights playing strip poker under the influence of the local, very foggy looking, Scrumpy cider would be any sixteen-year old boy's idea of heaven, believe me. Yes my heart raced but for entirely different reasons and for a few days, anxiety was the furthest thing from my mind.

Erica was the love of my 'then' life, but after two years I was told that her parents gave her an ultimatum: 'Him or university? It's your choice.'

What would any grade A student choose at this point? University, of course, and the relationship ended abruptly and my heart was broken. I spent months grieving and begging her to come back to me but she fought my advances, admitting that she still loved me and that 'I would always have a special place in her heart' but that wasn't enough for me. As a result, my self-confidence nose-dived into a sea of self-pity, anxiety and sadness. I couldn't see a way of retrieving my torn heart.

As a result, I made a complete fool of myself on a number of occasions as she enjoyed dangling a carrot occasionally, torn between wanting me back and the decision she had made. It became apparent that she had a new boyfriend but that didn't stop her from visiting me for 'a little more than a hug' occasionally and proclaiming her love. I never obliged, even though I still wanted her back; I had boundaries regardless of how sad she had made me.

She had put me through hell, my anxiety was back with force and I wasn't ever going to allow her to hurt me again. I had trusted her once, but the trust was gone. The panic attacks came thick and fast as I searched for the reason, searched for level ground. Where once there was focus, now there were nightmares, sleeplessness, panic, fear and sadness.

Dad and me

My relationship with my father was tense. I loved him unconditionally and he was my hero, however, he felt it necessary to keep an eye on everything I did and I felt undermined and suffocated. Although, perhaps a manifestation of my anxiety? Was this any different to the way all children feel? Was it done out of concern for me? I knew that I felt unwell and unhappy because of so many factors and I felt out of control and bored with everything around me. I felt unfocused, unchallenged and directionless.

This had a definite affect on my anxiety and I knew that I was disappointing mum and dad in so many ways.

I feel that I have always disappointed my family: this is, perhaps, partly due to the seemingly manic way my emotions have controlled my actions and partly due to the enormous crash which results from the meeting of a creative mind with that of people who are so 'über-practical'. The problem was that to everyone else, the solution to my problems seemed so clear because from their perspective life is simple but from that of a tumultuous, anxious mind like mine, nothing was simple and everything needed to be difficult, somehow embellished to interest me. . . I felt hungry for data but controlled by fear.

Please don't interpret my description of my parents' mindset as negative, while it was not right for me in so many ways, it works for them and millions of other practically minded, structured and successful people. It just wasn't me and the conflicts it caused were inevitable.

I didn't love my parents any less, we just didn't share this psychological mindset and this made me sad, it still does. I am the way I am and I have never intentionally made things difficult for anyone and it must have been so horribly frustrating for them to watch me make so many decisions that they would never have made. That all said, I don't think I've turned out too badly under the very negative circumstances I endured.

I was sad because it made the practicalities of cohabitation fraught but equally, because it prevented, or limited, close interactions that should be experienced by a teenage son; the same interactions that my brother now still enjoys without conflict.

People like easy interactions regardless of the truth behind them. It's easy to hear 'I love that idea' than 'I would do that differently', even when the alternative idea is presented with love, thought and reason – even when, ultimately, the alternative would produce better results.

Making money and having fun

I always worked to make extra money. I packed potatoes, worked on a pig farm, worked for dad and worked in a shop. I couldn't sit still and needed to work, initially to fund my expensive tastes in music and clothes, and then to fund nights out and girlfriends. One thing was sure though, I was never a follower, I couldn't bear the scrutiny; I needed freedom of choice and definite goals.

I had worked in the local hospital as a volunteer and loved it but my medical career wasn't to be. I used to watch surgery as mum assisted the surgeon to remove varicose veins, repair hernias or remove a pilonidal sinus. I loved it. I wanted to help people. I wanted to save lives and make a difference. Most of all, I wanted to choose a career that enabled me to learn constantly without ever reaching the end of the process. I needed intellectual food to fight the boredom that engulfed me when I didn't receive it.

I decided that art was a far simpler option and gained a conditional place at St Martins School of Art in London. The only condition was that I took a nine-month foundation course at a local art school – so I joined up before receiving my exam results and started the course at the beginning of September.

Just after finishing my A levels, a guy at school, Julian, invited me and five other guys from school to stay in one of his parents villas in Tenerife. I went out expecting it to be fun, sun and girls, but these guys had a different idea completely. They saw it as an opportunity to drink, drink, drink.

On the second night, Julian decided to take us all to a nightclub, so off we went to Playa de las Americas, dressed like characters from *Miami Vice*, sporting the most wonderful highlighted mullets. Julian knew exactly where to go, or so he thought, so after a ten-minute walk through hoards of holiday makers we ended up at the foot of some steps with a purple awning with 'Club de Nuit' written in gold framing the way to a night of fun and girls. On entering we were offered drinks by a very friendly bartender, which we accepted and drank leaning on the bar like seasoned drinkers. At eighteen, what did we know? Pretty much nothing. The alcohol measures in Spain are probably four times the quantity and halfway down our glasses things started to get a little blurry.

Suddenly music started, a purple curtain swished back and out of the back room strutted six gorgeous women wearing basques, stockings and very small underwear. Of course, six eighteen-year-old lads thought they had died and gone to heaven. *These must be the stage act,* I thought but they were headed straight for us and within seconds were straggling us on our bar stools, breathing into our necks and causing all six of us to truly panic.

Ian looked at me and mouthed, 'I think they're prostitutes.'

One of the other lads heard him and said, 'I don't care.'

I looked back in pure horror and said, 'I'm off'.

With that, all six of us sprung up and ran, with the club management in hot pursuit. Making it to the safety of another nightclub, we laughed until we cried. Slightly inebriated we ordered drinks. Shortly after a fight broke out on the dance floor as a huge northern girl punched her boyfriend and then knocked out a girl she thought he'd been flirting with.

Eight hours later, I sensed the warm sun on my face as I woke. Opening my eyes slowly I allowed them to adjust to the sudden burst of sunlight. Trying to move, I realised that I was outside and as I sat up, it came to my very panicky attention that, not only was I in someone's rose bed, but I was completely submerged in water with only my face above it.

Somehow, nobody ever admitted to knowing how, I had been placed in a flower bed, had a hose pipe fed up my right trouser leg, through my shirt, around my neck, back down through the shirt and down my left trouser leg. The water had then been turned on as I lay sleeping. The flower bed, which was about twelve inches deep had filled with water and I had slept, bobbing up and down on it all night, only through pure luck, not turning over and drowning.

My relationship with alcohol changed that night.

The holiday was not at all fun. It mostly involved one of the guys getting a brand new Jeep written off, alcohol, no sleep and childish pranks.

On my visit to the art school of my choice in London accompanied by my dad and brother, I was scared. Something deep inside me knew that I was never going to live in London; I think I played the part well though, shrouding the fact that it was all an act to impress my parents and the fact that my anxiety on the tube train was almost overwhelming, but neither my brother nor my father had a clue.

The familiar tightness around my throat, the sense of being suffocated, a light sweat and nausea haunted me all day and was amplified many fold by the one-on-four interview I endured with a group of middle-aged art lecturers who scared me to death. I was so scared in fact that I took home someone else's portfolio and left mine there, which resulted in a long trip to swap them back two days later.

The problem was that my conscious reasoning was always two steps in front of my actions and the actions would very often take a while to catch up.

While others were stepping off the tube train, concentrating solely on how to do so without being killed by a rush hour crowd, I was already considering distant possibilities about everything else which resulted in me being left behind like a gormless sheep, lost in the fog. I think it was this that caused my father to be so frustrated. He knew I wasn't stupid, but he just couldn't understand where my mind was most of the time. He is a practical man, intelligent and logical to the last and to see me wandering around in a dream must have been very frustrating.

If I could honestly tell you that the dream was due to brilliance, I would, but it wasn't. I was more scared and confused than brilliant. I do believe, however, that all the time this turmoil was weaving its way around every neural pathway in my confused mind, things were happening to 'fine tune' my intellect. I believe this now because I haven't only witnessed this in myself, but in nearly every single anxious person I have ever helped. It's like a light going on. Everyone says the same thing post recovery: 'I feel enlightened somehow – I feel like I have developed another sense – I am so much more intuitive'.

Emotional intelligence is present in every sufferer and causes there to experience a physiological change in the circuitry of their brain that can be achieved in no other way. I believe that those changes are a form of emotional and intellectual enlightenment forcing the advanced development of the human mind; just expedited by the anxiety disorder.

I don't believe that even recovered anxiety sufferers have maximised their intellectual potential, but I do wholeheartedly believe that they have opened an intellectual door that never closes again during the course of their life. It is a doorway that leads to far deeper experiences of everything around them through a hyper-sensitised nervous system wired from every nerve ending in the body back to a colossal bundle of advanced and massively developed circuitry in the brain – super neuroplasticity and a finely tuned and augmented connectome.

I have no physical evidence for this theory, but I could tell you ten thousand stories that would demonstrate its existence 100 per cent. This is also what I have experienced since recovery and, even as I write this, my mind swims with ideas and strings of thought. Is it any different from the experiences of other creatives? I don't know. I am not able to calibrate with others or compare intellect effectively. What I do know is that usually, in any given situation, I seem to have the problem solved or at least be along way along that route, before others have even considered the options. That's not to say I am a literary genius, my words come from my heart, not honed literary perfection or 'parrot fashion' learned data from textbooks.

Am I always right? No, of course not. But I am always focused and prepared when many others need to be primed for longer. I seem to always 'pull it off' when the odds are against me.

The anxious mind

It stands to reason that if the brain is a biological 'learning machine', constantly soaking up information received through our sensory organs, and that this information is categorised and pigeon-holed in our brain for future reference unless the brain decides that the information is only required short term, in which case it discards it. As information is stock piled, our intellect grows and providing we have the skills, which enable us to access the information when required, most of us use that information coupled with simple logic and experience to problem solve.

Imagine now a mind that is oversensitive, which receives massive hits of information, embellished by anxiety. It receives thoughts associated with fear, 'what if thoughts' of catastrophic consequences, inappropriate, but seemingly real nonetheless. These are 'risk assessments' made using sensory data to decide on what appropriate action to take in any given situation. Your brain is constantly building anxious scenarios deep within your mind; it is filing away these thoughts and experiences, building your stockpile of creativity, information, imagination and experiences.

Your mind is expanding exponentially with every thought, while, next to you, sits a non-anxious person with remnants of thoughts about their day swimming around in a mind, which would never send an EEG machine 'a humming'. As their thoughts rest comfortably in the armchair of their brain, yours is like Tokyo on market day.

Your brain is taking in data. It either stores it or discards it. The neural pathways, physical wiring within the brain structure, are being modified, pruned and discarded or replaced. This process is constant, whether you're awake or asleep. You are constantly evolving in a small way as your mind is modified in order to modify your interaction with your environment.

Getting fit is a perfect example of the way, through repetition of physical activity, you can condition your mind to control your internal organs more efficiently in a given environment. Day one, running a mile makes you out of breath, but as the days pass, the run becomes easy as your brain modifies the interaction between the heart and lungs to work more efficiently at this new level of activity causing you to become 'fit'. This happens constantly and, in some cases, like fitness, you can *force* it to happen.

You see, you *can* manipulate your subconscious, despite what psychologists might tell you, but you cannot do it verbally, which is why CBT and other talking therapies are often so ineffective in the treatment of high-anxiety conditions. You can't verbally reason with your emotions. CBT also assumes that thought precedes the emotional response, which is wrong and this is the core reason why CBT is for the treatment of anxiety related conditions flawed as a psychotherapeutic technique.

If emotional response and autonomic systems are to be adjusted, this can only be achieved by modifying incoming sensory data; this is how we cure anxiety disorders using The Linden Method. We change the way the brain responds (more specifically the anxiety response), by changing the data it receives. You'd think that would involve time, effort and focus ... but it doesn't.

My anxiety grows

Whilst worrying about attending art college in London, I was still reeling from the split with my girlfriend. My anxiety had worsened. I always felt a sense of heightened anticipation about everything I did and felt anxious if asked to travel any distance from home or to accompany someone in their car.

Since as far back as I could remember, even back to when we lived in our old Victorian house when I was just two or three years old, I can remember having a very disturbing, reoccurring nightmare. I mentioned this previously but I just want to underline its significance in the context of my anxiety disorder.

This dream would haunt me through the day and even when I wasn't directly thinking about it, the sense of fear and anxiety that it would cause would be ever present – a morbid feeling and a sense of impending doom.

This dream was often accompanied with a sensation of extreme size misrepresentation. For example, I would feel that anything I put in my mouth felt extremely large or something I touched was perceived by my brain as incredibly small. I believe now in hindsight that these were the confused experiences of anxiety but back then, they were ever-present thoughts and sensations, which, at the time, seemed perfectly normal to me. I don't ever remember telling anyone about these sensations.

As I matured, the mangle dream came to me less and less, but the anxious feelings remained. I don't believe there was ever a time when I felt completely at ease or contented. In secret, I felt scared and alone and in public I was a source of fascination to my closest family members who couldn't comprehend the behaviour, which led me to lack focus, make strange and irrational decisions and react so erratically or inappropriately to things with which everyone else coped.

My perception and experience of the world around me was very different to everyone else's, of that I am certain. It was this sense of fear and self-doubt that drove me to be serious and shy.

I needed someone to take control for me, but that need was buried so deeply in my subconscious that even I had no idea that it was there. My behaviour was that of a needy child, even as a young adult and, to a certain extent, I think, some of that remains with me today, but now I am a family man with a business and responsibilities, which satisfy that deep desire to be loved, nurtured and supported. I think it's still there but now it is superseded by rational thought, structure and focus and I feel mentally balanced, well and capable.

I am not totally sure whether everyone feels this way deep down and that these feelings in me have been brought to the surface by my heightened sense of reality. Perhaps it's a 'man thing' and women are, in fact, correct; we are all immature little boys who can only focus on one thing at a time and are fascinated by boobs and their penises. That can't be true can it?

I mean, boobs are great but, in truth, my experience of being a man has so little to do with constantly thinking about sex and soccer for 99 per cent of the day. Anyway, I much prefer a shopping trip and a massage and I can't stand football!

Whether I was at home, at Boy Scout camp or at school, my craving for intellectual activities, which would challenge me far beyond my capabilities, drove me to produce a long succession of absolute failures. However, my satisfaction lay not in a positive outcome but in pursuing the potential for success. I just needed challenge; the outcome was irrelevant really, it was all about the pursuit. In every failure there is at least one valuable lesson and as I collected lessons, the mistakes reduced.

Most people would feel undermined and negated by their failures but I actively pursued activities and ventures which would almost certainly end that way, all in the name of giving my brain something to 'chew on' without which, the ghosts of the anxieties I had tamed beneath the thin cloak of my subconscious mind would break free and control my every waking moment.

Writing this, I realise that this is the first time I have put words to my feelings. Until now, I couldn't find the appropriate vocabulary I needed to give those secret feelings the credibility they deserve. I couldn't find a way to communicate them to other people, to you, who deserve to know that they are not alone; that there are people, like me, who have a direct insight, through a very special 'extra sense' into the world beneath the façade of your life, your thoughts and your anxiety troubles.

In the deepest possible sense, we are connected by a common fear of fear, so strong and yet so futile, so damaging and yet so inappropriate and so preventable.

OK, mine has gone. I no longer experience inappropriate anxiety and I lead a normal life but every day I see new clients feeling exactly how I once felt and I watch them as they too become anxiety free and continue on their life paths unencumbered by inappropriate fear.

My school days were racked with the haemorrhaging anxiety, which was bound up tightly in my brain and every sinew and muscle in my body. I was told once that every cell in our bodies is replaced every seven years and it was, therefore, my hope that the fresh 'replacement cells' would mean that I was no longer 'me' and that the new manifestation of me would have discarded the anxious habit as they fell from my body.

What a dream, a fantasy built on false hope and a complete misunderstanding of the theory, but it comforted me... until the seven years passed and I was still, very disappointingly, me.

I never looked in the mirror and saw something I liked and this has been the case for most of my life. It is only now that I look in the mirror and see a great dad and a loving husband, before I just saw squirrel eyes filled with fear.

I now know that living life isn't about re-enacting a scene from *Waiting for Godot*, we aren't waiting for anything and if we do, we miss it!

We aren't here to focus on the 'human condition', we are here to utilise the fact that it exists as a wake-up call, a kind of invisible and yet ever-present stop watch to remind us of the necessity to focus on those things which fill our time with fulfilling activity and achievements which give us a sense of who we really are, what we want to become and how we want to be remembered.

Everything else is just window dressing. Our legacies are written by us.

CHAPTER SIX

Art School BS

ALCOHOL AND DRUGS have never been my 'things' but this place was riddled with people who were there for the ride. Lecturers who'd clearly fried their brains on substances, students who were playing at being artists, pretending that what they were doing had meaning and if it didn't, they found some weird justification.

I stood by and watched people aimlessly throw paint, melt things and bend scrap metal and plastic, and after three days of that, dinking huge amounts of coffee, smoking cannabis and a few pints at lunch time, they'd ponder on all it could mean and come up with a justification. I heard one girl say to the tutor, justifying the plastic and card mess she'd created, 'It represents the pain of menstruation.' What? She'd told me the previous day that it was a representation of a storm. I didn't get it at all ... not just her work but also any of it. My work was relatively attractive, structured and controlled and was created to be so.

So I started the one-year foundation course I had to do in order to get to St Martins. Well, what can I say? In certain circumstances the saying 'those who can do and those who can't teach' couldn't be truer. My experience of art school was one such example.

In my opinion, there were probably only two people in the entire college who had real talent; the others justified their untidy and sometimes illegible scratchings using the words of art critics.

If it has an understandable visual narrative, it's art, if not, it's a justified mess ... that's it folks! I didn't fit in as you might well imagine. I was unacceptable to the drug-taking, cigarette smoking, shit-speaking art fraternity and they made that very obvious.

I appreciate *all* art, pretty or ugly, I 'get it' but don't allow me to watch you to create it over a number of days during which the justification and explanation changes a hundred times and then, when finished, stand in front of me and tell the tutor that it has fulfilled your initial intentions. At least have the dignity to say that it turned out OK considering you had no clue what you were doing.

Tracy Emming's bed I, kind of, – get it ... Hurst's Polka Dots – get it, a tampon glued to a piece of blue drain pipe ... I'm struggling.

I wanted to do graphic design, as you may have already guessed and eventually work in advertising, at least there, people were pulling together visual and intellectual resources in order to create something that would appeal to the masses – affect their lives in some way and create a response albeit for crass commercial reasons. It still looked nice.

I wanted so desperately to go to art college in London, but if I were to get there, I would need to tolerate another eleven months of torment from the brain addled hippies masquerading as tutors and the constant bombardment of anti-graphic design I endured.

Then there's London. How would I cope with the isolation, maddening crowds, travelling, social life and moreover, the almost definite lack of funds I would have to endure amongst my silver-spooned, co-students.

I couldn't do it so I left college, letting down my parents and more importantly, myself. I didn't know what I wanted to do, but whatever it was I had to create an income to avoid the unavoidable conflict I would endure.

Real life

Every morning I would be woken early and asked what my plans for the day were. Asked to buy the newspapers and scour them for jobs, and to go to the job centre and rightly so.

My anxiety levels had risen considerably and the girl I was seeing, who was two years older than me, wasn't helping matters. She was a good-time girl who needed me to earn money in order to fund our active social life. She was a nice enough person but she was sex mad and money crazed.

I eventually found an advertisement for a property sales job based in Cornwall about 200 miles from home and after a very fast interview I was employed by them as one of their first 'time share' salesmen.

I travelled to Cornwall by train and had to stand the whole way. The train was packed and no one got off 'till we reached our destination. Four and a half hours standing on a train isn't pleasant let me tell you, especially when you are surrounded by over a hundred children under twelve on their way to a school outward bounds course in St Ives. My anxiety was horrendous. I almost wished I were back at art school. Had I made a monumental mistake?

When I finally got there, I found that my first few days at work were more about acclimatising me to massive quantities of alcohol than learning the job.

The first night was horrible. After being forced to drink spirits till I threw up by a sixty-year-old American, we had to walk over half a mile to our log cabin in the 3 feet of snow that had fallen during the six hours that we'd been bar bound. I opened the door of the bar and as the cold night air hit my face, I felt the blood drain from my face as I fell, semi-conscious, from the top step into a snowdrift. At least, the cold snow helped me regain consciousness quickly and I dragged my weary and very drunk body back to the log cabin where, for the remainder of the night, I walked rings around the sofa sipping black coffee for fear of dying from alcohol poisoning. That was in 1987 and I haven't touched alcohol since.

My anxiety was massively increased by my experience in Cornwall and I remember becoming quite panicky while in a nightclub. The increased and intrusive self-awareness, which overwhelms many sufferers, had raised its head again. All I could do was focus on was the distance from home, the lack of trusted people around me, my perceived frailty and the anxiety that was starting to leach into my life again.

It feels almost as if you belong somewhere else, as if you are living in a parallel reality where everything is identical to your true reality but there is a strong sense that there is something wrong, something unidentifiable but out of sync.

I always felt as if something was about to happen, like I was about to discover the truth – I guess this is the anticipation experienced by every anxiety sufferer, a fear of nothing and of catastrophic consequences based on nothing. These sensations are manageable to a degree but they leave the sufferer in a sort of limbo, existing but not living.

During the time I was in Cornwall, I think this was around two weeks, my girlfriend had spent her time when not working, with my mother. She had told her repeatedly how I was 'the one', which seemed incredibly forward and also premature to me but I went with it, but two days before I was due to return home, she decided to sleep with one of my work colleagues who she had been introduced to on the day I left. I only found out because I heard the guy bragging about it. I was so unaffected by this which surprised me.

The ultimate sin committed, there was no turning back for me and I entered into a period of higher anxiety. The job lost its appeal and the company was focused on relieving elderly people of their life savings. The job became a joke and I decided to seek other employment elsewhere and after a few weeks in early July, I was interviewed for a job with a local carpet manufacturer. I did get the job but decided to enjoy the summer by working on a beach in Wales selling ice cream from a traditional ice-cream van. I travelled to Wales with Damien whose family were from South Wales.

Pendine Sands, ice-cream vans and Germans

We had so much fun, marred only by the underlying fear that leached into my existence. I did feel anxious most of the time but the energy of youth pushed me forwards in my pursuit of a level of success, which would repair the damage I had done to my dwindling reputation in the eyes of my parents and wider family.

I was always embarrassed by my actions. I had very little conviction in what I did and always felt scrutinised and criticised for anything I did. What proportion of these feelings was justified and which were embellished by my inappropriate anxiety is still unclear but I do feel that I was unfairly judged.

I suppose I now know what anxiety sufferers endure and how the fallout from the thoughts and sensations can affect the family dynamic but I also know that, sometimes, others are to quick to judge and that judgment isn't always measured. People can be cruel and selfish as well as misguided by superficial 'symptoms' and behaviours.

My philosophy is that everything is worth doing regardless of outcome and even now I regard even my complete and sometimes extreme and expensive failures as a success on the Charles Linden sliding scale of life experience. I have less now, which is positive and I take less risks than I have previously but I still believe that nothing comes without some level of inherent risk and that things worth doing, nearly always, carry a certain level of risk.

You see I believe that even those things that fail in terms of the outcome which was planned at the start, have value in terms of the lesson learned throughout the exercise.

Someone once said that 'the most successful people in the world have had many previous failures', which I believe to be very true. Without the experience of failure, how can anyone learn how to minimise the risk of failure during the next venture?

Without a benchmark for or an indication of 'what *not* to do', success must be based on luck or someone else's failure and experiences. Life is a learning curve and any sophisticated task undertaken must be achieved through trial and error or experience. To me, this makes sense, however, because this process had to be experienced by me, rather than past on by others, I was considered stubborn or in some cases, immature or idiotic in some way.

I was constantly being criticised for not taking advice. I always took the advice; I simply chose not to use it in most cases. I didn't believe for one second that I knew better, I just wanted to try things out or myself without living my life through other people's experiences.

My brother is a whole different kettle of fish, which made things worse for me. We are so different: he was prepared to be guided, formed and lead; he accepted and acted out the advice that he was given. Even though I was criticised, ridiculed and belittled, I had conviction in what I wanted, even when what I wanted resulted in extreme disaster in some cases. Ultimately I was always able to accept my failings, say sorry when appropriate, pick myself up and move on to the next scheme ... some hare-brained, some sensible but most unsuccessful.

It's better to have tried and lost than never to have tried at all; at least that's the philosophy I'm sticking to and till now, it's worked OK for me. (The same is true of love by the way.)

Did these failures contribute to my high anxiety? Maybe, but they were the result of my personality, my drive, my ambition and my relentless wish to be remembered. I couldn't and wouldn't change that then, now or in the future; it's what I am.

So, there I was, sunglasses on, shirt off, selling ice creams to the good people of South Wales. Driving my ice cream van up and down the sands, avoiding small children and stopping at the slightest glimpse of young female flesh, which usually turned out to be pale, spotty and not at all appealing, but then, the British coastlines aren't particularly famed for an abundance of Californian-style beauties.

I was a young man on a mission and while I tried to behave normally, I recognised in me the anxieties that I had felt in my early teens, the same behaviour, which was now causing me to avoid tiredness, alcohol and girls.

Damien and I decided that we would buy a couple of toy guns and pretend to the girls in the local nightclub that we were undercover drug squad, a good plan, if a little childish.

To cut a very long and boring story short, I ended up meeting a couple of German girls in a nightclub in Saundersfoot, one of which, I thought was pretty and interesting. Patci (short for Patricia, pronounced the Italian way), was a sweet girl, her friend was a little bit, how do I say this tactfully ... well, too German, for me. She was nice enough but my God did she know what she wanted and she wasn't backwards in coming forwards to tell you either. In fact, truth be told, she scared me. Patci on the other hand was 6 feet tall with long blonde hair and she was nice, seemingly unapproachable, but nice.

For some reason, when my friends found approaching girls difficult, I found it easy. People don't scare me and even approaching dignitaries or famous people is easy for me when others shy away, the polar opposite of what others with anxiety experience.

Patci scared the wits out of everyone else but was a challenge for me. We spent a few nice days with the girls and, in-between selling ice creams on the beach, had a lot of fun until Patci told me that she was leaving to go to London for a few days before returning to Germany and asked me if would I like to join them?

I didn't know what to do. My friend would have been deserted in Wales and I was having a good time but, ever the adventurer and out of necessity to further my horizons, I decided that I would go. Damien was OK about it. He knew me better than anyone and still does actually. He is still one of the best people I know, even though we don't see each other as much as we should really, but he is loyal and kind and a great father to his lovely children, which always impresses me.

Damien is one of life's great blokes, a go-getter that gets crap from everyone around him because of his focus and forward- thinking mind. He, like me, is a self-made builder, architect and businessman who gets criticised by people for his constant advancements. Greed doesn't fuel Damien's quest or mine for more... the need for fulfilment and the quest to create our own legacies are behind everything we do.

I set off on the 200-mile journey to London the next day, not knowing where I would sleep or where I was going to find any money. The anxiety inside of me fired me on. I can remember feeling very lonely during the journey and the guilt I felt for abandoning my best friend in Wales attacked the very core of my conscience. I knew he would be fine, but I have always had a very strong sense of loyalty and nostalgia, and anything that upsets it causes deep sadness in me – almost on a cellular level; it affects my soul.

New horizons

So, there I was, with a few pounds in my pocket, heading blindly towards London and my destiny with a bag full of damp clothes and half-a-tank of diesel. Bloody fool.

What was awaiting me? What was expected of me? What the hell I was doing was a mystery to me, but, somehow, it seemed the right thing to do at the time.

I arrived in London and headed straight for the address Patci had given me. On arriving I found Patci and her friend on the step outside building looking vacantly around them. I think they were both pretty shocked to see me there, probably not as shocked I was though. Perhaps they thought I'd cramp their style. Perhaps they were disappointed.

We decided to head into the city, the girls had always wanted to go to Kings Road for a drink. How was I to know that their taste wasn't as cheap as I had hoped; two very expensive cocktails later, with a massively depleted savings fund, we left the bar and I now began to panic. First, I really was completely penniless now, and second the girls were hungry and hopeful that I would buy them a spectacular meal at a top restaurant. Needless to say they were disappointed and fed up ... let's leave it at that!

We visited all the top London sights over the next few days – all the free ones at least. They too had very few financial reserves and were just grateful for the free tour and transport. Patci and I clicked, she was a nice girl but I was still deeply affected by the split from my first girlfriend, I needed the friendship at least.

My anxiety was at a low ebb and they were totally unaware that, beneath the surface, I was feeling pretty intimidated and out of my depth.

The girls returned home to Germany and I returned to my parents.

Patci was clearly sad to leave me and the next few months became an exercise in telephone conversations and letter writing, which culminated in her revealing to me that her home life was quite strained and that her mother, who sounded like a complete maniac, was making her ill.

I was due to start work at the carpet factory in September but by mid-August I decided to visit Patci in Germany. This trip was a relief at the time, I felt under pressure to get a job and conform at home and just wanted to do something productive for me and not just to satisfy other people's need for my fulfilment. It wasn't me to toe the line.

After the weekend trip to Heidelberg, I decided to move to Germany permanently and on the following Monday I did.

CHAPTER SEVEN

Germany

Patci met me at Frankfurt airport, I was anxious, but she calmed me. Her father, Walter, was a massive man, 6 feet 6 inches tall with hands the size of a car steering wheel and a voice to match. He was a gentle giant, his voice soothed and reassured me, and I immediately felt a sense of trust for this man who was generous and kind in every way. In fact I later felt very sorry for him and what he had to tolerate.

Patci's mother, Dita, had wild hair that she sometimes wore in a bun. The hair was grey and framed her constantly startled-looking face. She wore blouses, but not the conventional way, as she tied the sleeves around her chest like some sort of native binding.

Dita said she had allergies, particularly to smells and ran around with her fingers tightly pinching her nose closed in case she smelt my aftershave or deodorant. While I was staying with them, I found that the whole family used a perfume-free soap; and not only did we have to shower with it but it was also used to wash dishes, clothes and hair. The soap was actually a shower gel but in that household it was used for everything and God forbid you should smell fresh and clean. To me, the place smelt of cat faeces and sweat.

She treated Patci like a child and had convinced her that she was something very special indeed, despite their fairly modest lifestyle, because she was from an 'Adliche' family, a family of nobility.

Patci told me that when World War II broke out, the family were evicted from their castle, after her father was killed for his political anti-Nazi views. Dita and her mother were then forced to walk from, what was then, East Germany to Heidelberg to escape and the Nazi soldiers abused Dita during the journey.

Although I can't know what this must have been like for a six-year-old girl, I can see blatantly why she ended up with such peculiar and sometimes disturbing patterns of behaviour. She had later, apparently, dated Prince Rainier of Monaco and become something of a socialite but this had just served to fuel her belief in her own importance and her ability to convince Patci that she too belonged with the nobility and not with a struggling British expat.

When Patci had visited London the previous year, she had been taken for a day trip to the zoo, and her mother had decided to call every phone box in the zoo with the hope that a German would answer. Believe it or not, as Patci passed a ringing phone box, her teacher had decided to answer it and passed the phone to a highly bemused and embarrassed Patci. I now recognise that Dita suffered with multiple obsessions and compulsions and that her 'vapours' were panic attacks.

The only thing Dita didn't seem to be allergic to was a ratty little Maltese dog with a bow in his hair called Andy, who served not only as her friend but also her bodyguard, snapping at anyone who got within two feet of his guard.

By now, you are probably in little doubt as to why my anxiety became embellished, and I have to admit that some especially unusual people surrounded me as I negotiated my life. I must attract eccentricity – it does embellish life though.

The language school

The following day, I started at a language school, which was set up in order to bring foreign students up to a standard of German language that would enable them to attend Heidelberg University.

My father had said that he would pay for the course but within just a few weeks retracted the offer. With my anxiety increasing, Patci's father agreed that he would pay the fees for me, which was very generous. At the time, I didn't realise what this commitment would mean, but soon it became apparent that shopping, working at their snack bar, collecting and delivering a variety of weird and wonderful items from around central Germany, but mostly, selling ice cream at their ice cream shop, would serve as recompense for his generosity. I didn't mind. I was just grateful to be allowed to continue learning German.

I met a great American guy at the language school, which had previously been the Schloß Hotel. Perched on the hillside neighbouring Heidelberg Castle (Schloß), this hotel had once been the pride of the town and also the place where Mark Twain had lived during his time in Germany. In fact, I lived in his room for over six months.

Joe was a great guy from San Francisco in California of Italian descent. Half Italian, half Native American Indian, Joe was and still is one of the nicest people I know, and during our time at the language school, we helped each other out of some sticky situations a number of times.

The school was inhabited by people from diverse backgrounds: Palestinians, Iraqis, Chinese, Africans, they were all there – some completely sane, some not so.

Many of the students would defecate in the shower, use the toilet walls as toilet paper and drink cannabis-laced coffee while discussing death, torture and politics. The Margaret Thatcher hating Palestinians scared me and on a number of occasions I felt threatened, especially when one attacked me in the kitchen holding aloft a carving knife and screaming, 'Die Margaret Thatcher Fucker die.' If it hadn't been for Joe walking in behind him and grabbing the knife, I may have, indeed, died in the name of a politician I knew nothing about, for a cause I knew nothing about, while making myself a cheese and pickle sandwich in a language school in Germany.

Students would think nothing of paying for their studies by performing sexual favours for money. Some starred in pornographic movies, others just performed in the railway station toilets. They weren't gay, but 'a job's a job', they would tell me.

Once I caught an infection, probably due to sharing a toilet with other students in this germ-infested dump. For two days I lay unable to move, paralysed by a gut parasite. If the emergency doctor hadn't knocked down the door on the third day I'm not sure what might have happened.

The school may have been a dump and the students a mixed bag of misfits from around the globe but there were some good teachers and a handful of good students too. I made friends with a Brazilian called Chico who had arrived at the school unannounced wearing a pair of flip-flops, shorts and a T-shirt. His only possessions were a toothbrush, toothpaste and deodorant, which he kept in a clear plastic bag.

Chico not only paid his way through the language school by working in kitchens, but also funded himself through university by working a number of jobs at night and weekends. He was an inspiration to me and still is actually and a really nice guy to boot. He eventually gained a doctorate in chemistry and then I lost touch with him. I've since looked for him but with no success.

The death of PB

My grandfather PB died after a very short illness while I was in Germany. I had no idea that he was so unwell and the blow came from nowhere. Everyone else in my family had the opportunity to see him before he passed away but it was too late for me and this is a regret I carry with me still.

Around this time, my first girlfriend was also calling me and asking me to go home to her. Something inside of me wanted so deeply to return home, I was missing my family and the sadness of losing PB was cutting deep. I had no money but nana Kay bought me a plane ticket to return for PB's funeral. I decided that I couldn't stay in England. I knew that yet another failure added to my escalating list would have just given people renewed ammunition with which they could continue their ridicule of me and my achievements. So, I returned to Germany – against my better judgement – but in support of my mental health. I was becoming more anxious and now started experiencing my intense fear of contamination and infection again. I started hand washing again. It wasn't constant but the ever-present fear of catching HIV was gaining momentum and dominated my thoughts no matter what I was doing. My OCD and Pure O were escalating.

I needed money and in a bid to fund my existence, I decided to become a street artist. I built myself a display case, which could be quickly folded in case the police turned up to move me on. Inside the case I constructed shelves with cord retainers behind which I placed my watercolour paintings. I would draw a pen and ink sketch of a scene around Heidelberg and the castle and then photocopy this onto artist's watercolour paper which I would then hand paint.

I produced a range of images, photocopied them many times onto watercolour paper and sat on my stool colouring the paintings through the year, come rain or shine. I sold many of my paintings to tourists and made a good living, enough, at least, to buy myself out of the language school, complete my studies there and buy a car.

The police arrived on a number of occasions, sometimes with warrants, but each time I managed to escape arrest by folding my shop in a second or two and diving into the nearby bushes or running back to the language school. My pitch was next to Patci's father's ice-cream shop, which was useful to him when he needed a hand and also meant that our friends would be treated to free ice cream occasionally.

Armed with the German language

A new gallery was opening at the end of Rorbacher Straße in Heidelberg and the owner had seen some of my paintings that local people had commissioned. Most of the subject matter was Mediterranean architecture and sea views with a twist –the twist usually being a strategically placed orange or lemon. They were nice paintings, not particularly adventurous but commercial.

The gallery owner asked me to produce thirty paintings in just a three-week period and, despite feeling very pressured, I delivered thirty-two paintings of various sizes, but most over 4 foot by 4 foot a day earlier than expected. He was delighted and the exhibition was a success, I sold sixteen of the thirty-two paintings and the rest stayed in the gallery for a while. I sold four more and the rest were taken down in preparation for collection.

In the time between taking the paintings down and collecting them, apparently there was a flood in the gallery and the rest were destroyed. Their insurance would not pay for them and I lost them all. I never saw them again and it was my suspicion that they went elsewhere to be sold. I've never found out.

Christmas came and I desperately wanted to be at home with my family but I couldn't afford a ticket home, so I spent Christmas alone at the language school. Patci and I had decided to split up, although we did get back together again shortly after, but at that time, I hadn't seen her for over a month. My friend Joe was away and the other students, most of which didn't recognise Christmas anyway, were either working or away somewhere over the break.

At home, my family took it in turns to host Christmas lunch at either my parents' or aunty Jackie's house. Nana P always made a fuss about Christmas and this resulted in a number of family arguments and some nasty fall-outs. This particular Christmas, my aunt was hosting celebrations with her husband John. John didn't like me and I have no idea why that was. Unbeknown to my family, knowing that I was hoping to speak to everyone by telephone during the day, John decided to unplug the phone at the socket to prevent my call from being heard. It wasn't until my parents became suspicious and my dad checked the phone line that they realised what he had done.

In the meantime I sat in my room wondering why there was no answer when I called, which I had been doing every fifteen minutes. My room was a five-minute walk from the telephone kiosk and I must have walked there twenty times that day. I expect you would understand the sense of loneliness and desperation I felt that Christmas day.

For some reason, I have always had a deep sense of self; a profound sense of my humanity, the frailty of our species and the sensitivities of myself and my inner child; this day brought home just how lonely life can be and how some people must feel much of the time.

I had been working nights in an Irish pub, mostly for fun but also because the extra money paid the insurance on my car. I met many strange and wonderful people at that pub but one, a middle-aged man with a very peculiar personality, made me feel very uncomfortable indeed. He had befriended a woman with definite psychotic tendencies who would discuss suicide and murder openly. My anxiety was raised every time she entered the pub.

On one occasion, I received a telephone call at closing time from this man who begged me for help. I drove quickly to his apartment. He let me in and asked me to sit while he fetched his girlfriend. I sat on the bed nervously as he left the room only to return with her, both naked. She forced herself on me as he stood and watched, clearly aroused by the situation, which he had orchestrated. I was not interested. In fact, these two people were the least attractive people I could ever imagine becoming sexually embroiled with and I wasn't about to have sex with a man, or even have one present!

I panicked and left afraid and confused.

I did see the man again the following week when he asked me to open a high-class brothel with him. Of course I refused. About six weeks later his girlfriend committed suicide and he stopped visiting the pub.

I served and cooked food at the bar for another six months and then left to work for a Dutch American man who supplied stock to the US army stores. This was to be an adventure.

CHAPTER EIGHT

Diamonds and Socks

Poorly equipped with an old Citroen BX and a cheap suit, I was sent off aged twenty to restock the US army, navy and air force bases around Europe. With a wide range of goods including jewellery, socks, ceremonial swords and other trinkets, off I went blindly into the unknown and loaded with over $10,000 of samples in two cheap plastic briefcases.

My sales area encompassed Germany, Holland, Belgium and Italy including Sicily, not the average sized sales territory but how was I to know that? I had no idea that these countries were so far apart, they seem so close together on a map!

I travelled the length and breadth of Germany, once a month going to the US air force headquarters in Belgium and Soesterberg in Holland and in between, visiting every army and air force base from Bremer Haven to Munich, from Nurnberg to Kaiserslautern.

Once every six weeks, I would drive from Heidelberg, down to Stuttgart and Munich, down through the Alps through Austria, down the East coast of Italy to the 'heel' of Italy visiting Bari and Brindissi, down the coast road under the boot of Italy's instep, onto the toe and across on the ferry to Sicily.

Sicily, that's a strange place – miles and miles of nothing but heat and rock and the occasional puff of smoke from beneath your feet where mount Etna smoulders waiting to explode and engulf every living thing. At least that's how it felt. I couldn't help wondering why people would want to live on an active volcano, my anxious mind didn't understand why people would bring up a family on an island that could, potentially, end up like Pompeii, which I also visited regularly on my journey.

The island is circled by a thin band of towns and villages along the coast roads, and by the time I reached the US base near the centre of this smouldering dust bowl I had stripped down to nothing but shorts as the sweat poured from me.

The gate guard checked my pass and immediately advised me to drive straight ahead, park and jump in the pool. The pool was like marine soup, packed from poolside to poolside with equally sweaty, overheated humans, but what a relief, I thought I would cook.

Having convinced the US government that what they needed most on Sicily was a bigger stock of sweat socks and gold jewellery to add to their already overloaded inventory, I left the hospitality of Baskin Robbins and continued north to catch the overnight ferry to Naples.

In Naples I would rest for two days visiting Ischia, Capri or Pompeii to inhale the culture of ancient Italy and the smell of rotting cats and dogs, which, for some reason, they neglected to remove from the roadside when they had been killed by a passing Ferrari.

Rested, I would travel north through Rome and across the country to Venice. Again, I would rest for a day and always try to make a trip across the lagoon by boat taxi so that I could experience the tingle as it turned up the Grand Canal, a vision that cuts through the foul stench of raw sewage to provide an experience second to none in my estimation. The surreal seconds as the familiar dome appears flanked by the most beautiful architecture and gondolas bobbing up and down on the water, is a sight that must be seen to understand its impact.

All this time, I felt more than anxious but somehow I kept moving forwards.

After a break in Venice, I would then continue back up through Austria and Germany, north to Berlin through Nurnberg. Reaching Bremen I would then descend back through the north of Germany ending at Frankfurt. The whole trip was so long that it really wasn't worth measuring but what I do know is that the Citroen had 14,000 miles on the clock when I collected it and after twelve months it had 39,000 and the weird thing is that I can remember probably every single one of those miles.

Exciting and frightening times

During these trips, I experienced some very strange, exciting and frightening things and now, looking back, my only regret is that I didn't have anyone with me to appreciate it and bask in the excitement.

On one occasion, I had just passed through the Brenner Pass into Austria when I rolled down the window to let some cool air pass through the overheated interior of the car. As the window opened, a gust of wind knocked my Ray Bans clean off my face and I watched as they disappeared in the rear-view mirror, bouncing into the central reservation of the autostrada. The air was blue I can tell you, those glasses were carefully placed into their case each time they were removed from my nose usually but this time they were being scraped and battered to oblivion by a frying-pan hot length of Italian road. I pulled off the motorway at the next stop and filled the car with petrol, picking up a cheap pair of sunglasses without which I would never have been able to continue the journey. With over 3,000 miles ahead of me, a car without air conditioning and an external temperature of thirty-eight degrees, there was no way I could have coped without my sunglasses, a supply of freezing water which became hot in less than an hour and my Bermuda shorts, which travelled with me everywhere and had started to look a little worse for wear.

While filling my car with petrol, I noticed a small very dark-skinned man filling his moped with petrol at a neighbouring pump and thought it wise just to check which exit to take in order to get back onto the autostrada towards Venice. The man was friendly enough and spoke broken English, which was very useful considering my lack of Italian fluency only surpassed by my Spanish! The small, raisin like man directed me to the correct exit and I drove away confident and hot.

After, perhaps, another hour I decided to stop for a toilet break and to replenish my near boiling supply of foul tasting water, which had rolled under the passenger's seat and burst open filing the car with the smell of damp, warm carpet.

I turned into the rest area and parked up.

As I approached the small shop I noticed a very familiar looking moped and standing behind it, a very familiar looking raisin-like man who turned and said, 'Hello man, I see you again,' in his broken English.

The momentary notion that I had been abducted by aliens, had lost time in some other twist of the space time continuum or, more likely, I had finally gone 'fruit loop', made me dizzy and I sat down on a nearby bench.

I had driven perhaps 75 miles in searing heat on a busy autostrada and a small man on a moped had beaten me to this rest place and had time to buy himself an espresso and drink it prior to my arrival. Either he was Einstein's understudy who had used his boss' data to construct a time machine from Italian farmyard paraphernalia or, as previously stated, my mind had finally broken in the extreme heat and under the ever-increasing weight of my fear.

I sat at the rest place for a further hour or so pondering the explanation, which I never found. It was weird at best and all I could think was that I had somehow taken a wrong turn or that I had spent much longer at that last stop than I thought. I was tired, maybe in that alone, somewhere laid the explanation.

My anxiety hit the roof. I was hot, alone and now to add to the mental turmoil, also confused. Logic told me that something was amiss and for the first time in my life, I was unable to find the answer to an every day occurrence. My heart raced and I recognised suddenly the sensations of panic that I hadn't experienced since my early teens.

Of course, at this point I was still able to rationalise the response, not realising that my subconscious was busy building the monumental structure of neural pathways, which lead to the development of a true, full scale, anxiety disorder. My brain was re-learning, fear-building behaviours as physical rewiring deep within my brain and I was unaware of it – and more importantly, powerless to do anything to stop it; or so I thought. The panic subsided but was replaced by an overriding memory of its sensation that burned an ever-present belief that it could return into my conscious mind at any time ... the fear of fear started to create more fear.

I continued my journey and visited the rest of the stores with the enthusiasm I always displayed, hindered only by the occasional burst of adrenaline, the occasional palpitations and a deep realisation that something wasn't quite right.

Having done my tour of Italy, I ended up, as usual on the edge of the lagoon in Venice. Parking my car, I grabbed my case and jumped onto a nearby boat taxi. In my anxious haste, which resulted in a kind of 'emotional blinkering', I completely forgot two vital things: first to notice and remember the number and name of the car park; and second to take my valuable samples from the boot of the car.

Landing at St Mark's Square I headed for the nearest café to buy a bottle of water and sat for a while, as was becoming a tradition as I experienced all these great things alone, to breathe in the atmosphere of this mystical place, spoilt only by the click of tourists cameras and the flash of gaudy, golf style, clothes.

Bad news and a panic attack

I always stayed at a small family run hotel off the north side of St Mark's Square in Venice. The family was kind, very friendly and always fed me well and talked to me, sometimes until the small hours of the morning.

I had just finished my dinner and decided to use the phone in the lobby to call my parents, just to let them know where I was. I had spoken to my mum the previous day and detected a strange tone in her voice. I had asked for an explanation and she had said that she had argued with nana Kay, which I thought was particularly odd, as they never argued.

There was no answer at home so I called nana Kay. I knew she would give me an answer. She sounded odd too, saying that everything was fine and that mum was out with my dad. But I knew there was more to this than I was being told and my anxiety started to rise as I telephoned other family members who all sounded very vague.

I sat in the hotel lobby for a while feeling very worried indeed. At around 9 p.m. I decided to try my mother's number again and this time she answered. I detected nervousness in her voice that I had never heard before as she told me that my father was in intensive care having had open-heart surgery for blockages in his arteries. Apparently he had been unwell for a week and they had operated three days ago. Whilst he was recovering well, she suggested that I shouldn't fly home specially and that my brother and his girlfriend were looking after the business by answering phones in the office for my father and everything was under control.

I felt the room begin to spin and I fell to the floor as the hotel owner ran to me and helped me onto a couch in the hallway. I experienced my first full-blown panic attack and I thought I was dying as I clutched my chest and struggled to breathe as sweat dripped from every pore. My mind flew into 'what if' thought patterns, flights of fancy fuelled by the anxiety, which gripped me.

I couldn't make sense of what was happening to me, it seemed so real but I also knew what it was. It didn't make any difference though. The panic attack gripped me for over an hour as the hotel owner and his wife sat with me. They were so lovely and I owe them so much.

As I sat there a grim reality hit me. I was in Venice with a car full of expensive merchandise and my only way home was the drive back to Heidelberg – ten hours of driving alone.

What is a panic attack?

I now know that these catastrophic thought patterns are the psychological catalyst of the anxiety response; once they start, they self-perpetuate in the subconscious mind until the conscious mind stops the cycle or the flight or fight response subsides as adrenaline is used up.

A panic attack is like a steam cooker valve. As adrenaline is released, under normal circumstances, in which true threat exists, it is used up to flee from or fight that threat effectively. However, with an anxiety disorder, where no true threat exists, it isn't used up, so the body activates a panic attack in order to use up that excess adrenaline safely. Panic attacks are an unfortunate side effect of adrenaline release and are, in themselves, completely harmless. They feel horrific and the symptoms can be far-reaching and frightening.

As the panic attack gripped me I thought, 'What if I pass out? What if I make a fool of myself? What if I die? What if I never see my family again? What if I end up in hospital? What if my heart explodes? What if ...?' *All* risk assessments activated by the anxiety response. *All* designed to help me to assess a real risk. *All* designed to save my life. *All* completely harmless, but *all* making me and every other sufferer around the world *feel* like the end is nigh.

These thoughts are the foundation for the anxious cycle, anxiety disorders and obsessions, which can lead to OCD and many behavioural aspects of anxiety disorders such as agoraphobia. They are the thought patterns that underpin inappropriate anxiety in every case. At the time, as the realisation hit me of what 'might have happened', or, 'what could have happened' to my father, the 'what if' thoughts took over and my mind was swimming with a tangled mass of anxious thought, it all seemed so real, on a cellular level.

Secrets, secrets and a dreadful journey back

I was devastated that my family had hidden this from me and that no one respected me enough to tell me what had happened; he is my father too and I felt side lined by my mother and brother. They would dress it up as 'protecting me' I am certain, but the truth is, I believe, that I just wasn't a symbol in their equation at the time.

Mum later told me how sad she had been that I had made the decision to move to Germany and leave the family. I didn't see it that way at all. I wasn't leaving to get away from them. I was leaving to get away from myself. I never felt happy as me and I believed that going to Germany was an opportunity to forge a new me, to become self sufficient and to return as a more rounded, organised and mature man instead of the dependent object of ridicule I believed I had become.

As soon as I started feeling a little better, I packed my case, thanked the hotelier and his family, paid my bill and ran to St Mark's Square to take a taxi boat back to my car. My heart was banging and I could feel the anxiety surging through my veins.

Of course, it was only at this point that I realised that I had no idea where I had parked the car and also that I had left all the valuable jewellery samples in the car boot, but as I stood there, tears rolling down my cheeks, heart racing, my taxi driver from the previous day spotted me and shouted over to me a crazy moment of synchronicity or fate that saved me when I needed it.

I was so thankful as he took me over to my car. I have no idea what I would have done had he not seen me. There are probably at least a dozen car parks around the lagoon and I couldn't even remember from which direction I had entered the Grand Canal.

Safely back at my car, I closed my eyes as I opened the boot, slowly opening them to find the samples still safely in place.

I drove up through Northern Italy at speed, my heart racing pretty much all the way. I drove up through Austria, stopping for petrol at the Bremer Pass and then directly up to Munich, a drive I would usually savour – the Alps are so imposing and beautiful, so this section of my journey was always the one I most looked forward to. Not this time.

It was 2.30 a.m. and I was so very tired. The remnants of my panic attack were still coursing through my veins and nervous system. Occasional electric shocks across my chest and down my arms teased me, making me jump. My heart fluttered and my mind raced but I felt a little more in control as I drove past the Munich turning counting every minute that passed. The last 250 miles of the journey were always the longest and driving when I was so tired in a section with no road lighting was draining me.

Suddenly I noticed that the road had become much darker but I continued, struggling to see the autobahn ahead of me. I started to realise that my headlights were dimming and over the next mile or two, they went out.

The panic rose up in me again and as I struggled to see the road ahead, the realisation hit me that I was alone and my car was dying around me; as the fear engulfed me, my engine died.

CHAPTER NINE

Munich and My Alternator

I SAT IN MY CAR and cried for about an hour whilst my heart beat shook my clothes. The darkness engulfed me and I had no idea where I was. I hadn't seen a road sign for miles and only a handful of cars had passed me in the last hour. It was at this point that a mobile phone would have served absolutely no purpose at all because at that point I realised that any help was at least seven hours away from me, my family really didn't need a call from me in the middle of the night and I knew that Patci couldn't have cared less.

I had no idea how close I was to civilisation or whether I could walk to fetch help. This section of the autobahn didn't have an emergency lane and I felt vulnerable sitting in the slow lane of a major motorway so I locked the car and went out into the night dragging my suitcase and leaving thousands of dollars worth of merchandise in the boot of my car.

I decided to climb the embankment first and look over the top but as I reached the top I realised that I was in the middle of a forest and couldn't see any light in any direction. I descended back onto the autobahn and walked in the direction I had been travelling hoping that a passing vehicle would take pity but they didn't.

I started to imagine what could happen as if I were living a scene from a Stephen King novel. The panic gripped me but as the adrenaline was released in constant stream, it was being somewhat utilised by my appropriate fear, dragging the suitcase, clambering up embankments every hundred yards and the tension I could feel in every muscle as I prepared to fight my murderer.

After walking for perhaps half an hour, I saw small flickering lights in the distance against the shadow of a mountain and after a further twenty minutes of suitcase dragging I reached a small village where I decided to knock the door of a neat looking guesthouse.

This was one of only five buildings in the village, the others being a post office, two houses and a petrol station. No one came to the door despite the urgency of my knocks. The adrenaline coursed through my body and I began to feel angry. By this time I was on the verge of another panic attack and I had never felt so alone in my life. I curled up into a ball and lay there in the porch, crying sporadically till dawn.

All I could think of was dad lying in his hospital bed, my gold-laden car, perhaps 5 miles away on a deserted motorway and the hunger and loneliness that made me feel like an abandoned puppy in a sack. I was so in touch with my humanity and it hurt.

Stranded

The next morning, after negotiations, the village garage retrieved my car for me and it took three days to get the offending part from Munich to repair it. The alternator had burnt out, as had I. Money had run out, I had nowhere to sleep and no one to talk to. Despite phoning various people to request assistance, I had to sell some of my jewellery samples to pay for cheese, bread, water and the alternator. It was the worst three days of my life up to that point.

Having spent five days driving home to Heidelberg, my father was out of hospital and taking long walks. My boss was furious about the samples I'd sold and even more furious that I had wasted so much time driving home. He didn't show an ounce of understanding or compassion for what I had been through. Having been severely reprimanded for my actions, I told him to stick his job 'firmly up his arse', and returned to Heidelberg penniless, alone and desperate to go home to England.

I had no money to buy a plane ticket and in truth, despite wanting to be there, I didn't want to go. I felt completely side lined, disregarded and undervalued. I had been informed that my brother and his girlfriend were 'running the business', it was said in a way that spoke volumes to me and although I was, at this point, unaware that my suspicions about my position in the family were justified, deep down I knew something had changed. Something was telling me to keep away.

More than all of these mixed emotions, I was scared of seeing my father. My anxiety was building by the day and felt incapable of facing dad after his ordeal. I became more concerned that I was feeling unwell due to an underlying heart condition that I was ignoring and seeing dad, his surgery scars, his weight loss and having to confront him after I had been absent during his distress made me scared beyond belief. I just couldn't face him and while I felt increasing shame, I couldn't explain how I felt to anyone, they would never have understood.

I now know how anxiety about health affects people and recognised, from that moment on, that it formed the basis for much of my anxiety and obsessive behaviour.

I still feel ashamed today but it still troubles me to address the issue and the biggest problem is that I really don't know whether there ever was an issue but, for fear of opening up old wounds, I stay silent. In my mind I know, however, that I couldn't have faced my fears back then.

Panic attacks gripped me three to four a day, day and night. The derealisation overwhelmed me too and I had a constant sense that despite being alive, I was living in a dream.

A new job

I was then offered an opportunity to sell cars to the US forces and after an interview on the seventeenth floor of an office block in Frankfurt, which I reached by walking up all thirty-four flights of stairs due to my anxiety about lifts, I returned to the UK to do a course in sales technique.

I felt so stupid, so vulnerable and so childish; I masqueraded as a confident, mature adult but beneath the surface I was a scared and timid child struggling to remain sane.

I enjoyed the course until day three when we started a module in role-play. I went to pieces, silently. I would sweat, shake and lie awake all night worrying about the next day's activities. My anxiety was escalating but beneath it all was a deep fear that I didn't know what was going on in my body and mind, all I knew was that something didn't feel right and there was nothing I could do about it.

After seven very long days, I flew back to Germany and was transported to Kaiserslautern in Western Germany by minibus. We were treated like a commodity rather than a valued team. I felt like one of a flock of sheep as we were herded in and out of training sessions, offices and seminars in which we learned how to extract money from potential car buyers in the quickest possible time, mercilessly asking for deposits using whatever 'close' was necessary. I felt uncomfortable with this but I needed the money and it was my last chance to build some stability into my life before being forced to concede failure and move back to the UK. I felt cornered and alone again, isolated by circumstances and anxiety; my fear of failure spawned anxiety and the anxiety was growing daily.

I spent the next eighteen months selling cars. My office was the furthest back in a long building. The door was situated at the narrow end of the building and the three offices consisted of partitioned cubicles, which meant that any potential client would need to negotiate the sales equivalent of the medieval gauntlet in order to reach the safety of my office.

The guy in the front office was a young but excellent salesman called Keith from Nottingham and, while we got on socially, our working relationship was love/hate and, in truth, more hate than love most of the time. Keith would stand at the door to our offices handing out brochures to every passer by and grabbing each 'prospect' as they entered the building and, more often than not, get a deposit before anyone else had a chance to make an offering to the poor unsuspecting soldier, who had only popped onto the base for a few bottles of Bud. Keith was the star salesman, his unsuspecting prey would undergo every sales tactic in the book until he got a signature; he was almost robotic in his regurgitation of the sales patter. He lived it. He looked middle aged in his long trench coat and grey suit and tie. His slicked back hair, close shave and soft voice were the perfect tools for his assault on every passer by but he was good and made a huge amount of money.

The next office was occupied by a wonderful black American ex US forces major called Willie; a very entertaining character who looked forty but was actually seventy. His attractive French wife who was in her fifties really had to keep an eye on Willie, he had a roaming eye and a penchant for young women, the further under thirty the better. His sexual conquests were revealed in a string of sordid stories and his charm was only surpassed by his flirtation skills. Willie was a playboy as well as the Ford agent who formed the second stage of the gauntlet, which was our office.

Every morning I would arrive at 8 a.m. and clean my show cars come rain or snow then I would open up the office and set to work checking orders and doing the banking in the on base bank. I did OK, in fact I got salesman of the month on a number of occasions and I think my bosses were impressed that I sold anything at all given the competition and the layout of the offices. I know this is an irrelevant fact at this point in the story but I was the only salesman ever to sell rustproofing and extended warranties on every single car I sold, a fact of which I am very proud. It doesn't seem like an important fact now but the reason I mention it is because although we were taught to sell cars using tactics and closes, I sold cars through friendly debate, problem solving and honesty and it worked.

Desert Storm was tough on everyone with the soldiers away on duty in Iraq, the base was more or less empty of uniformed personnel and selling cars was almost impossible. I requested an air drop onto the front line but my bosses refused, the team had been oversubscribed by eager salespeople wanting to monopolise the 'Front Line Market', after all, what else has a soldier on active duty on the frontline got to spend his pay check on?

I was relieved not to go eventually, my anxiety prevented me from doing very much at all and I began to wonder why I had volunteered; I think, inside of me somewhere was a notion which said that if I carried on regardless, eventually everything would fall back into place. How wrong I was.

One morning I was entering the base and the military police checked my car for explosives with mirrors on poles. As I sat in my car an MP checked my ID as I felt my heart rate building. Slowly I started to hyperventilate as the MP looked on thinking, probably, that I was a suicide bomber or terrorist. Eventually they let me through and I headed for my office to splash my face with cold water. I had experienced a sudden burst of deep-rooted fear about the situation in Iraq, an almost cellular fear of the unknown, the future and war that I had never experienced before. It was almost as if I was looking my fate in the eyes and my mind wouldn't defocus from the obsession I was developing. The fear was so deep, so profound and yet so inappropriate that I began to fear for my sanity. I was becoming obsessed with my mortality and there seemed to be nothing I could do to defocus.

New business

During the desert conflict, Keith and I were propositioned many times by bored and sex-starved American wives and one morning I arrived in my office to find a very pretty young woman in stocking, suspenders and bra, minus her knickers, lay on my desk. As I quickly got her dressed and ushered her out of my office, I was met by another army wife on her way in to 'buy a car'. This happened quite a few times over those months; I won't mention names but certain sales people gave into their charms but I never did.

My boss broke away from the company we worked for and was keen to develop his own business. He already had his own insurance brokerage and sold some vehicles from there too so the transition was easy for him. I was an agent for Chrysler, Jeep and Harley Davidson and he wanted to expand his offering to those manufacturers, so he offered me a position selling for him.

I had been doing a lot of business with the Canadian Air Force in Germany and had subsequently developed a good relationship with the base commander who had invited me on base on a number of occasions to hold car shows and Harley Davidson days in a disused aircraft hanger. These shows had always been a major success and I felt comfortable with the Canadians, they were quite British in many ways and we generally had more in common.

I decided to propose a business partnership to my boss Tony, which involved a constant presence, if not on the airbase, then just outside of it. This meant that I could retain the great contacts I had made and capitalise on being the first ever agent to have been given permission to trade on the base; they even issued me with a Canadian ID card.

Tony was very keen and soon the car sales centre was opened, which was quickly followed by our oak furniture centre next door. Tony was a great boss and a really good friend who I regarded as a father figure. He was forceful but also reliable and good to all his staff and friends, and he helped me out on a number of occasions during the early years of my anxiety. He never discovered the cause of my strange and seemingly timid demeanour but he seemed to understand me even though, sometimes, I would feel as if he thought I was a little silly or childish.

After I left Germany I searched for Tony in order to explain what had eventually forced me to leave but could never find him. In 2010 I was on friendsreunited.com updating my page and there to the right was a list of 'People you might know' and top of the list was Tony's name. I messaged him saying, 'Are you the Tony I worked with in Germany selling cars?'

A day later he responded and told me that he lives in Mallorca, Spain and unbelievably about 10 miles from where we holiday each year. We met and have remained in touch since. Such a lovely guy and his partner is such a lovely person too.

Tony was the reason I stayed in Germany so long and also the reason I remained relatively well; his confidence, despite sometimes being edged with a little Yorkshire 'plain talking', was confidence building and exactly what I needed back then.

The impending crash

I was working long hours and the journey from Heidelberg to Lahr, the furthest Canadian base from home, was about 60 miles. Most mornings I was at work for 8.30 a.m. and I wouldn't leave the office till 8.30 p.m. and was working seven days a week. I knew I was pushing myself too hard and the signs were becoming more obvious and less sporadic; I was becoming unwell and I should have known better but the momentum of duty and commitment was too strong and I was carried along on a wave that was soon to crash to the ground.

The car sales started to decline as the Canadians started withdrawing troops from Germany and my anxiety became centred on my financial situation. My parents came to visit for a long weekend and they lent me some money for which I gave them two hand-signed Salvador Dali lithographs as security for the loan. I had bought for my apartment earlier in the year but money was getting tighter by the week.

(

CHAPTER TEN

Food, Autobahns and Girlfriends

I BEGAN TO WONDER whether my diet was causing me problems. I had been experiencing some indigestion on and off for some time and I had put on weight, which was uncomfortable and frustrating. My weight fluctuated; I was a comfort eater and the only time I was at my ideal weight was when I wasn't in a relationship.

I decided to enlist the help of Patci's father who was a well-known natural health practitioner. He suggested that I take some food supplements, one of which was sillenium, an extract from the starflower plant, which was supposed to help stimulate the metabolism. He also suggested I take some vitamins and cut down on fatty foods, which was obvious really.

I don't know whether you have ever been to Germany but their diet seems to be solely dependent on fat as the prime ingredient, and what I could buy locally, which could help me lose weight while provide the nutrients I needed, was fairly restricted.

My diet was ridiculous. For breakfast I would eat green beans, for lunch I would have dry crackers with coleslaw salad and would often miss dinner because I got home so late. Patci never cooked, prepared lunches or went shopping for us, but that is a whole different story, which I will explain shortly.

I started losing weight but I felt really unwell by now and my godfather David was due to visit me, which worried me because I didn't want him to see the physical and emotional mess I had become.

One night I was on my way home, pondering the future when I hit traffic jam about 6 or 7 miles into my journey home. The jam didn't move for three hours and the occupants of the other cars decided to get out and have a walk around. Eventually everyone was out of their car wandering around chatting, swapping resources and listening to music on their car radios. I was feeling very unwell. I hadn't eaten and I felt faint; I had no food with me and there wasn't a shop for around. My heart was pounding and the fact that I couldn't move my car or go anywhere was scaring me.

I didn't have any means of communication, as this was pre-mobile phones. I started to become truly terrified and panic set in. I walked a little further along the autobahn but soon returned to my car. After about seven hours, I saw that there was a steep drop to a gate in a field about 200 yards from where my car was parked and although it would mean moving the cars into the slow lane in order to get to the hard shoulder and attempt to drop my car down a steep bank, I thought the time was coming where I'd have to take my chances. My anxiety, by this time, was though the roof. I was sweating and filled to the brim with overwhelming fear that was spilling out as panic built.

After eleven hours, it was 7 a.m. by this time and light enough to see track clearly, with a hundred or more cars as onlookers, I took the law into my own hands, opened the gate at the bottom of the bank and plunged down the bank in my VW Corrado, which grated and bounced as it hit foliage and rocks. The onlookers were amazed. Not only had I broken the law, a sin beyond comprehension by the majority of Germans, but I had risked flipping my car over ... why? They had no idea of the torment I was experiencing. I would have done anything to escape and really didn't care about the risk of arrest or death behind the wheel. In fact as I descended on the embankment, real fear gripped me and the adrenaline was used up, so the risk had created two positive outcomes, I was off the autobahn and my anxiety had reduced.

I hadn't done any permanent damage to my car, a few superficial scratches, which later polished out. On arriving home I was greeted by an increasingly familiar sight of Patci, drunk and asleep surrounded by wine bottles and empty plates. The smell was overwhelming. The sink was spilling over with dirty food plates and the bottom of the sink was filled with food matter that was rotting in the heat from the roof window above it and as I moved the plates I saw maggots moving around in the bottom of the sink. The smell of the apartment was like a bin in summer and I felt incredibly nauseas.

Life with Patci

Patci had two pet rabbits and when I was away, she would allow them to run freely around the house. Rabbit droppings were everywhere, thousands of them, rabbit food and sawdust was strewn all over the carpets as she would lie there at night, sipping wine, watching TV and playing with the rabbits.

She too had her problems. Her mother was driving her crazy and her internal battle with her own sense of achievement was really pulling her down. On a couple of occasions, I took her to hospital too discover what was going on, but to no avail.

I understood the problem. The constant pressure was bringing Patci down and she was becoming more dependent on alcohol and more depressed. My financial situation was partly to blame, I am sure. She was used to being provided with all the clothes she needed, a car, holidays and meals out but my income was sporadic, seasonal and at best only stretched to a few meals out at restaurants. I paid for our cars, a three-bedroom apartment, her clothes and a skiing holidays each year but it still wasn't enough. I was twenty-three years old and the weight of the world, my businesses, the bills and my own anxiety were crushing me.

A few days later, I came home to find her drunk again. This time she had stepped out of bed onto a wine glass and badly cut the sole of her foot, which wouldn't stop bleeding. We spent hours bathing it and bandaging it; she refused to go to the hospital and her mother, in her infinite wisdom, was advising her by telephone what to do. Eventually the bleeding stopped and she spent over a week in bed bandaged up. Her parents never came to visit, never helped her in any way and her mother just criticised and whined over the telephone at least twenty times a day. I had started being less 'respectful' and as my German language ability had grown so as to be about 80 per cent fluent, I was able to express my displeasure more effectively.

I told her exactly what she was doing to her daughter and, having never been spoken to like that before (because every one else bowed to her demands) she decided that I was the devil himself and that she would never speak to me again.

Die Putzfrauen Insel – The Cleaning Lady Island

We decided that we needed a holiday. I was scared to death, to say the least, but an old friend, Marc, had come out from England to help with the business and after I taught him the ropes, he seemed confident that he could hold the fort for two weeks while we recuperated in Spain.

I wanted to return to Mallorca where I had spent many holidays with my parents but Patci's mother told her that she shouldn't holiday on '*die putzfrauen insel*' (the cleaning lady island) because only common people went there. Ignoring her ridiculous claim, we went anyway.

After a very fraught flight out, during which the flight crew had to sedate me with Valium, we landed in Mallorca. Over the first few days, Marc's daily reports were positive and he seemed to be doing fine but on the third day he disappeared, completely! I called the UK and no one had seen him. Our friends in Germany couldn't find him. The office was locked and the car I had lent him was back on the driveway at home. Two days passed and we heard nothing.

Patci refused to return home and I couldn't blame her but, while I was losing money at work, relaxation was the furthest thing from my mind and my anxiety shot through the roof. I had an enormous panic attack while lying in the sun one day. It was horrendous and lasted more than three hours, exacerbated by the heat and by Patci's complete disregard for my wellbeing.

On day five, Marc reappeared in the UK at his mother's house. I think he had been there all along. He had jumped ship due to his high anxiety and posted my office keys and car keys through our letterbox before taking a taxi to the airport. Coupled with the anxiety and loss of business this caused me, we had to pay a hundred deutschmarks to open the front door to retrieve our only set of keys on our return. The holiday was a disaster and Marc offered no apology for his behaviour.

My godfather, David arrives

My godfather arrived for his visit soon after and unaware that there was anything wrong, I planned to take him for a boys' night out to the casino in Baden Baden and then on to a nice restaurant for dinner. Secretly I was terrified but I couldn't allow David to see me like that.

David was a man of very good taste, an intelligent and personable man with a wicked sense of humour and charming beyond words to women. I didn't take him to the casino because he was a gambler, but simply because it is the oldest casino in the world and it is beautiful. The exterior is exquisite but the interior with its baroque style mirrors and painted ceilings is a masterpiece of interior design.

I had just finished work after a long day and was driving home to meet David who had driven down from Frankfurt that afternoon. As I drove, my stomach churned with anxiety and anticipation; I hadn't seen David for over three years and I was worried on a number of counts, but primarily that he might see through the façade of fake confidence and sneak a peak at the mayhem that was going on beneath the surface.

David and I had always been close; somewhere in the relationship was a deep mutual respect and probably a recognition of like minds in many ways; we remained very good friends and until his sudden death on Christmas Day 2008, he would visit us at least once a week, offering support and encouragement. His advice and guidance with all business matters was invaluable and he constantly made us laugh at his antics, mostly around his love life. David wasn't an easy man to understand on an intellectual level, his sense of humour could offend the less aware. He never meant to offend, it was just that his sense of humour was clever, sometimes close to the mark socially and weighted heavily with sarcasm and to some people who didn't understand this kind of humour, nasty comments and ridicule are the last line of defence.

David recognised a problem in me as soon as my head was through the door. His concern was evident and David being David, within moments he was asking searching questions. I didn't want to talk about it. I had realised that giving my condition words tended to give it power too and, although David's intentions were good and deep down, I wanted to tell him everything, I was worried that I might be pouring gas on the flames and as it happens, I was correct.

After an hour or so we left for Baden Baden, a journey of approximately 30 miles. I knew immediately that things weren't right in the spaghetti of my mind; I could feel the adrenaline firing as I drove and electric shocks shot across my chest and down my arms. The familiar heaviness in my left arm and the ever-increasing heart rate meant only one thing.

My anxiety was exacerbated by David's presence ... trying to maintain control was causing me more anxiety and the loop was unsustainable.

I couldn't allow the anxiety to overwhelm me while David was with me but the inevitable happened and soon I was hyperventilating as the autobahn ahead of me twisted and turned ahead of me and the 'what if' thoughts bombarded my subconscious. I felt the familiar trembling feeling race through my body as the anxiety overwhelmed me and I had to pull over and get out of my car.

David raced around the car as I sat on the side of the road, head in hands, shaking, hyperventilating and panicking; I was scared beyond belief and I had no idea what to say David and every word came out wrongly like word salad.

David said, 'You look really pale. Are you OK?'

His good intentions were futile, the fact that he had vocalised how I looked was enough. This firmly reinforced that I was ill or dying and the sudden adrenaline release sent me flying to my feet as I grasped the railings of the autobahn bridge gasping for air.

David was scared, I could tell by his tone. I think he thought I was having a heart attack and his words confirmed that he didn't understand what was happening to me; but that was fine – how was he to know what to say or do after all?

The symptoms started to subside after half an hour or so and we continued the journey to Baden Baden. I was determined to enjoy the night at any cost. The anxiety was constant the whole evening and I couldn't eat at the restaurant, but I did my best to make David's visit as enjoyable as possible after such a bad start.

Later, we sat in his hotel room discussing the issues I faced, trying to get him to understand what I had been through.

I had been in Germany for three years and desperately wanted my parents to visit me. My brother and nana Kay had visited. In fact, nana Kay had stayed for two weeks once and saw what I had to tolerate with Patci, my job and lifestyle. She was worried to death but what could she do?

I believe nana Kay was around eighty-nine when this picture was taken. She stood five foot ten inches tall even at that age.

Now the anxiety was constant. My brain had adjusted; I could feel it. I felt as if high anxiety was now the norm in my mind and my body was reciprocating with constant electric-shock feelings, the heaviness in my left arm, palpitations and continuous, obsessive and disturbing thoughts.

David went home and I felt relieved. I no longer felt embarrassed by the obvious signs of anxiety but I was also filled with dread that I no longer had a sane person, on whom I could rely, within easy reach.

Isolation

I suddenly felt isolated, lonely and overwhelmingly sad. I had started calling home more regularly but my concerns fell on deaf ears. My parents and nana Kay, who had always been there for me, belonged firmly in the 'pull yourself together brigade'. It was difficult for anyone to understand what I was going through, I understand that, but it would have been nice to get a phone call once in a while to enquire about how I was feeling but they were few and far between. Anxiety sufferers often feel this way. It's an isolating condition on many levels.

Isolation comes from lack of medical help, the constant reminder from 'so called' medical experts, that the conditions are (supposedly) incurable, that no one, except other sufferers can ever understand how it feels, that family members don't 'get' that it's not self-inflicted, at least in the way they believe it to be.

Isolation also happens as sufferers withdraw from normal behaviours and activities, perhaps even becoming agoraphobic as I did. Isolation comes from the mental state that anxiety places a sufferer in, in which they feel captive of their thoughts and start to internalise their thoughts, focusing mostly on what is happening in their bodies and heads.

Getting worse

Monday morning came and I felt relatively well. I was feeling more positive about everything due to seeing David. He had that affect on me because he always seemed to know what to say to be supportive and this had given me a lift. I got up at about 6 a.m. as usual and drove to the autobahn where I pulled into a gas station to refuel. The morning was cold and wet; drizzling rain shrouded everything in grey. I opened the car door, swung my legs out of the car and the next thing I felt was something cold and wet on my back ... the floor!

My legs buckled and I hit the floor like a sack of potatoes.

As I sat against my car wheel the world spun around as if I was on a fairground ride. I shook visibly and my heart raced as three people rushed to help me to my feet, but I couldn't stand. Ten minutes later I was sitting in the back of an ambulance wondering what was wrong with me, and feeling very alone and terrified. The paramedics gave me the 'all clear' after about half an hour and an ECG. Of course there was nothing wrong with me, they diagnosed anxiety on the spot and I drove away embarrassed after thanking the people who had lifted me to my feet.

Things were getting worse. I was becoming desperate and decided that the best course of action would be to return to England where I could seek medical help and the comfort and reassurance of my family.

I told Patci immediately and she didn't seem shocked at all. I asked her if she would like to come with me but she declined and one week later I packed up my car with my most treasured possessions and drove to the border followed by Patci. I left behind an apartment full of furniture, electrical equipment and paintings, my other car and lots of accumulated treasures, which made up my home.

Mixed emotions overwhelmed me as the ever-constant anxiety made me focus on what awaited me in England so I also felt sadness at leaving Patci, who had been more of a companion than a partner for the previous two years at least. I felt a sense of relief as I drove away from my responsibilities, tinged with a sense of loss, failure and overwhelming sadness at leaving the home and country I had come to love.

I still feel a twinge of sadness when I think of Heidelberg and the fun and adventures I experienced in Germany. The German people are good, loving, generous and funny in their own unique way. I had come to love their eccentricities and admire their sense of style, design and ingenuity.

CHAPTER ELEVEN

Back Home to Family Bliss

HAVE YOU ever seen the film *Invasion of the Body Snatchers*?

Apart from obvious differences, which I won't go in to, that was the film set of a life I walked back into, or at least it felt that way. I will never know whether I was welcome back at the family home, without being joined to the Borg 'family collective'. As I mentioned before, no one can ever know the motivation behind other people's actions and behaviours. It would be so much easier to have first-hand insight into other people's thoughts and intentions. If we could calibrate our minds in some way, well this book wouldn't exist for a start, you would have already had the information as our minds exchanged data.

What I do know is that, unlike the 'Borg', the rest of my collective made me feel like my circuits had blown.

Now this isn't to say that there was intention or conscious effort from anyone to make me feel this way, although there may have been. However, the combination of my mindset at that time and the mindsets of the people I was rejoining made *me* feel this way.

Hunting for normality

Now I was back in England hunting for work. I decided to do a ceramics-restoration class. Nana P dealt in antiques and had requested that I mend certain items occasionally so, seeing a gap in the market, I decided to enrol on a course at a small restoration studio in a nearby market town. I enjoyed the first two days of the three-day course until disaster struck. On the second night, driving home in the wet, I turned a left-hand bend to find myself facing a small car on the same side of the road as me, which had over-steered the bend to compensate for a much too fast approach. I steered to miss him and lost control of my car.

My car hit the bank head on, went up through some trees and came back down onto the road nose first, flipping over twice lengthways, bouncing on the roof and coming to rest on all four wheels. I only remember standing on the road holding my head, which I had very badly cut when the car had hit the road. The car doors were sealed shut and the roof was flat onto the steering wheel. The windows were now slits and I had no idea how I came to be outside of the car.

My first thought as I stood there bleeding in the dark was *Why me?* The second thought was that familiar and deep existentialist notion that I didn't really exist and even this painful and disturbing event was just a figment of my imagination.

An elderly couple stopped, wrapped my head in a scarf and rushed me to the nearby village hospital and a trucker lent me his mobile phone to call home. I was covered in blood and I remember very little of the crash. To this day it remains a total mystery how I got out of the car.

A glued head, concussion and a written-off car later, I was sat at home feeling very anxious, dizzy and pissed off with my existence. Dad took me to see nana P but I was completely 'out of it', concussed and anxious beyond belief.

The next day, I went to see my car, which had been broken into overnight while in a security enclosure at a nearby body shop. The CD player, graphic equaliser, speakers and amps had gone, as had anything that could be removed from the rest of the car. The next night, the car disappeared and I never saw it again. The insurance company wouldn't pay up as the small print of the German policy stated that cars were only covered third-party while outside of Germany. The car represented all my savings so now I was broke, without a car and losing my sanity. Dad said that he would pay to repair the car and rescue some of my loss. But he didn't.

I couldn't finish the restoration class. The town I lived in, the people, the surroundings, it was all such a massive departure from the town I knew in Germany and this had a profound effect on my sense of wellbeing.

Living again in the UK, things like the food, the driving habits, driving on the other side of the road again, dealing with people's anger and road rage and bad attitudes served only to compound my anxiety. I was in Germany from 1987 until 1993 and, even though I worked with the armed forces, worked in pubs and travelled Europe, I never saw a fight, witnessed any anger, had a confrontation, got 'road raged', heard swearing in the street, saw young people misbehaving, saw drunk people throwing up ... and the list goes on. As soon as I returned to the UK, there it all was. It was quite a culture shock. I had forgotten what it was to be a British citizen and I missed the outdoor cafés, the coffeehouse culture, the simple, clear rules, and the cleanliness and organised environment I had grown accustomed to. OK, Germany wasn't perfect and there were exceptions, but the people were mostly scared of authority, knew the boundaries and respected themselves and others.

I felt displaced and alone again. I felt as if I would never find my place in life, like I'd always be wandering the Earth looking for my spiritual home. I had missed my parents and brother, but whether I had adjusted my own view of them, measuring it from a more mature standpoint or whether they had genuinely changed so drastically in my absence, I don't know. I just know that I felt alienated. I felt isolated again, even more so than I had in Germany, it all seemed so nervously embellished by being surrounded by those who 'should' love you unconditionally and feeling that you somehow aren't welcome.

I perceived a general sense of negativity when I was around. I felt like a houseguest who had outstayed his welcome. I don't think was a conscious choice by anyone, I just think that maybe over the years I had been missing, the gap I left had been filled and when I returned, no one knew what to do with me.

My anxiety-fuelled hyper-awareness was like living through a magnifying glass. My senses were so sensitised. I tried to get back into socialising and my brother 'set me up' on some blind dates but they didn't work out.

I met one of my brother's friends who was lovely, pretty and fun but she wasn't at the time in her life at which she wanted anything more than fun and, at that time, I just felt that I needed something with a more substantial foundation after so much uncertainty. We saw each other regularly for a while but we stopped when we both realised we needed something else.

One night in a momentary lapse of common sense, we went out and I drank beer, which ended in disaster and it was at that point I remembered the Tenerife incident when I was eighteen.

Culture shock

Arriving back from Germany was a culture shock but what amazed me was that in the five years I was away no one had moved on. The same people were propping up the same bars talking about the same things, remembering things that happened to us when we were sixteen, laughing about that time Robert drove through a phone box, or John got his willy out and won a bet with it. It was sad and depressing. Then they would ask me what I had been doing but quite honestly there was too much to tell them and they weren't truly interested in my stories about Germany, Italy, the Harley Davidson rally I created, the businesses I formed ... their interests lay in the comical moments in which their lives had been momentarily enriched and most of them only had these tiny experiences as the memories of a decade passed.

Despite the anxiety, the negative experiences and the loss I had experienced, my life had been enriched and my mind programmed by a massive and influential group of experiences that no one else I know has had. Despite it all, I was a better person.

After a long period of deliberation and anxiety, I decided that I needed to remove myself from the negativity of the UK. The weather alone was getting me down. The fact that I no longer had transport or anywhere to live was depressing and restrictive.

Having had so much independence and having had my own apartment with possessions, cars and the trappings of a fairly successful twenty-four-year-old, this was a disaster.

I decided to go to Mallorca for a few months, but prior to that, I decided that I would apply for a place at university. I knew that Mallorca wouldn't bring me the intellectual fulfilment I needed but I knew I needed to be somewhere else.

My job hunt had been blown by a number of rejections even though my sales performance was exemplary and I had out-sold and delivered the sales people at the dealerships. I was interviewed to the ratio of 4:1 and the rejections came as quite a shock and my hopes and spirits were dashed. Long term, this was to become a blessing in disguise but at the time I couldn't understand why a dealership would turn away an experienced and highly productive sales person who had not only equalled the monthly total sales of their entire sales team, but had never delivered a car without the extended warranty and rust proofing packages, had set up their own US specification vehicle import business with Chrysler, General Motors and Harley Davidson, and aged twenty had created car shows and showrooms on the Canadian bases. I was selling millions of dollars worth of vehicles every year but in the UK, no one wanted that.

I didn't have an inflated ego but I was realistic. I knew I could do the job standing on my head and after I was rejected by one garage in favour of a thirty-year-old bloke that I had known all my life, whose alcohol and glue-sniffing habits were probably behind his 'sleeping rough' look, I decided that 'enough was enough'. I was also later told by a car dealer friend of mine that the figures I had produced would terrify sales managers, hence the rejections.

My anxiety was OK. The doctor had prescribed another course of antidepressants and they seemed to be 'knocking the sharp corners' off my symptoms; a soporific affect, which gave me some respite from the most invasive sensations and thoughts. I now know that the bottleneck they caused was not a cure, in fact, far from it, and they caused massive problems long term. Knowing what I know now and having seen tens of thousands of sufferers use medication, I wish I had never let one tablet pass my lips.

Mallorca

I had met up with Marc again, yes the one who had abandoned my business in Germany . . . I am a forgiving soul. He too wanted to do something exciting with his summer so I asked him to join me on the trip and having secured a place at a university in Hull starting in October, we set off to Mallorca with two mountain bikes and a lust for fun. My anxiety was at a lower ebb but still ever present and the flight was a living hell for me. It wasn't about the fear of air travel safety, it was solely about control, not being able to leave the plane if I needed to and about the confinement amongst strangers.

We arrived in Mallorca in early May, and it was raining. In fact, it was torrential. Marc had been very nervous during the flight. Not so much about flying but more about being away from home and whether we would find work. His fears had distracted me somewhat and had opened a discussion about fear in general and it became very apparent that I wasn't the only anxiety sufferer on board that day. Marc's anxiety was pretty bad but at the time I had very little to offer him in terms of advice or reassurance because, secretly, I was worse.

Making our way to the resort where my parents kept a holiday house, the first quest was to find accommodation, which we found within an hour, in the form of a very cheap hotel room with two beds a small kitchen and a bathroom. It was fine for what we needed.

The resort was deserted for the first week and our desperate attempt to find work to fund our summer was in vain. We visited restaurants, nightclubs, golf courses and hotels but the season hadn't yet started and the weather was making the locals lethargic, even more so than normal. Nonetheless, I was there and very willing to work and, as always, I was very unprepared to take no for an answer.

The end of the two weeks approached and while I was hopeful that the following week would bring fresh hope with the weather, which was now hot and sunny, Marc was feeling down about the whole arrangement and I could see the fear in his eyes. In hindsight we had arrived too early. We should have waited until June but I still felt that I needed to get out of the UK and I think I did the right things. As for Marc, it was the wrong thing. He became very disheartened and didn't like the uncertainty. I had lived with uncertainty and fear all my life, it wasn't foreign to me to not know what to do next or where the next money would come from but it had made me resourceful and positive, he was just scared.

The return flights were booked as part of the package to get us out there and on the final night we were offered an opportunity to clean boats for the summer at the private yacht club in Santa Ponsa; an opportunity too good to refuse. The boat club is exclusive, filled with interesting people, not least pretty girls from across Europe and our boss was a really nice guy called Brian who was supportive, friendly and was prepared to pay us well. Satisfied that the summer would turn out OK, we went to bed after a meal of baguette and cheese.

The next morning I woke to find Marc had gone. He had packed his bags and bike while I slept, taken a taxi to the airport and flown home; Marc the deserter yet again, abandoned me. He must have been struggling emotionally. He is such a nice guy but seemed so timid and concerned. Despite my anxiety, I was able to do pretty much anything I wanted, not because I was necessarily stronger than other people but because I experience a massive and more damaging sense of dissatisfaction and loss when I give up. Failure is my biggest fear.

The summer was fantastic. I wasn't going to be the brunt of criticism about being unable to hold down a job, make a sensible decision or stick at what I started again. I knew my limitations and still do; I also know when I am not happy or fulfilled. I have always felt that life is a journey filled with compromise and knew that I should take advantage of the freedom while I was still single and without too many financial restraints.

I was only twenty-three years old but already had more life experience under my belt than the average retiree. It's all too easy to sit back and let life happen to you while you await the 'inevitable' thunder clap which brings all dreams and ambitions to realisation ... but trust me, if you wait for a storm, it generally won't come and if (or when) it does arrive, it'll be much too late to take advantage of the benefits.

I believe in being the storm maker, being the instigator of your fate and getting on with the task in hand as quickly as possible so that the next moment becomes free to try something else. In marketing terms, I believe in 'launching' the product as soon as it's complete, not when you have engineered and re-engineered it to perfection. When it works, do it. You can always 'fine tune' later. Too many people procrastinate, asking 'Should I or shouldn't I' or 'What if

...' Often, by the time you have prepared yourself for the perfect launch, the moment has passed.

Trust me, one day, the noose gets tighter and if you haven't done all you wanted to before then, the process is slowed down or even stopped by the responsibilities of life or unavoidable barriers and obstacles as you pass through life's 'gauntlet'.

Anyway, that's my theory and I'm sticking to it! To this day, it's worked for me and, despite the critics I have faced and the hurdles I have negotiated, I feel that my life has been enriched by my experiences.

Cleaning boats

In Mallorca, I loved cleaning boats with Gina, my partner in crime with whom I shared breakfast, lunch and smutty jokes. Her wicked sense of humour was a blast and we became good friends despite her taste in, what I perceived as, very weird men.

Gina had been hired eight weeks before me to clean boats and together we made a great team. Occasionally I would be asked to present a boat to a German client as I could speak the language, which was fun. Occasionally I would be integral in selling a boat and land myself a bonus, which would mean I could buy some new shoes or shorts to compliment the other six or seven items of clothing I possessed.

I shared an apartment with a chick magnet called Gary from Dorset. Nicest guy you could ever meet and a great flatmate. Strangely, we were born on the same day, which gave us an instant connection.

He would return home at 5 a.m. with two girls in tow, one for him and one for me but I was too shy and tired to get involved, which caused him and every other expat in the resort to conclude that I must be gay. I made friends with a great Scottish guy called John who was gay, and we had great times in the resort at night. He made me laugh with his camp humour and anecdotes. This friendship fuelled the rumour I am sure, but I had no concerns and it sort of protected me from my lack of interest in the ladies. I just wanted to have fun. I had no interest in getting into another relationship.

I lost weight, got tanned and fit and enjoyed every second of the six-month trip but I needed to start to consider what I would do through the winter.

I'd met a few girls throughout the summer and had a couple of holiday 'flings', one with a dancer from Manchester who was incredibly beautiful but also incredibly uninteresting despite her appearance. But I didn't want to complicate life with a new love and decided to keep firmly focused on getting to university.

I had hired a white 50cc moped to scoot around on and this served as a vehicle, not only, for my often tired-out body at the end of a twelve-hour day cleaning boats, but also as a vehicle for a more active social life, which often took me to BCM in Magalluf for a night out ending ten minutes before I was due to start work. This coupled with the occasional spliff meant that sometimes I wasn't as capable as I could be as I jumped from boat to boat.

One weekend I was invited to a party at a club in Alcudia. Realizing that Alcudia was in the north of the island, myself and my friend, Sharon, decided that we would jump on my moped and get to the party at about 10 p.m. that evening, We set off at 7 p.m., allowing ourselves enough time to 'chill' before we went to the club. Two hours later we were in Palma and by 1a.m. we were approaching Alcudia. Sixty miles from home and tired from our journey at 20mph on a knackered 50cc Honda, we entered the party, leaving an hour later to sleep.

The next day at 7 a.m. we started the journey home and on arrival, slept on the beach till it was dark. Sharon was a lovely girl but I am not sure she was very appreciative of my trip planning.

Recreational drugs

I just mentioned cannabis so I want to quickly talk about the experiences I have had with many thousands of clients, young and old, who smoke or have smoked cannabis.

Many people experience anxiety, panic, derealisation, depersonalisation and other anxiety related symptoms while smoking cannabis and once activated, these can perpetuate indefinitely.

I believe that the drug opens neurological pathways in the mind that activates an enhanced sense of risk. People with the predisposition to developing high anxiety shouldn't smoke cannabis, it's that simple and if they do, they risk activating an anxiety disorder. The commonly experienced paranoia related to smoking cannabis can be enhanced; paranoia is a risk assessment too. It may not feel like one, but it is, and this gives rise to a perpetuating cycle of activation of the emotion of fear.

Has permanent damage been done? No, not that has ever been evident but once the cat is out of the bag, it's tougher to get it back in. Of course, curing anxiety is what I now do and know it's simple, but when anxiety activates out of the blue, the sufferer can feel isolated and without support or guidance, this can be incredibly frightening.

Many people defend cannabis use on the grounds that it helps them to relax; indeed, we have had clients that smoke to overcome their anxiety unaware that the cannabis is activating it.

We have helped thousands of sufferers to overcome their cannabis related anxiety and they are no more difficult to cure than any other case.

New challenges

My parents came out to their house in the resort in mid-August and I told them that I was starting university in Hull in October doing TV production. I had been involved in forces TV in Germany and had found the challenge of programme-making interesting. Mum and dad tried to persuade me to stay in Mallorca saying that it suited me, but this just fuelled my belief that they didn't want me at home.

They believed that I would be better staying in Mallorca over the winter and perhaps getting a waiting or bar job until next season when I could recommence boat cleaning. Whilst I enjoyed the boat cleaning immensely, it was more a money earner than a career choice.

There comes a time when realisation hits: that we all need to feel secure and loved when we are growing up. I'd always felt cared for, except for the constant teasing and jaunts from my brother and the bullying at school perhaps. I can't say I ever felt unloved but suddenly at this point in my life I recognised very definitely that we are alone as individuals and that those who you believe are part of you, actually aren't. Now I wonder whether my somewhat sketchy sense of security as a child was actually a smoke screen and that all of my anxieties about life and my recurring nightmares were actually the result of nana P's weird taunts and the dynamics of my family in general. In hindsight, being referred to, as my mother's bastard by my grandmother probably wasn't nurturing, it and other family issues probably had a far greater impact on me than I was aware of at the time – who knows.

It only takes a change of heart, an argument a difference of viewpoint or a built in resentment to produce a dramatic sense of loss, of loneliness and of sadness that is invisible to others but so very damaging; this can manifest itself immediately or much later. I now recognise that the people around me did things and said things that damaged me and despite seeing the impact these experiences had on me, they seemed always to ignore them. No one ever dealt with the bullying teachers effectively. Sure, mum went into the school occasionally if a teacher moved my books or if she had instructed me to punch someone, but the wider and more influential issues weren't addressed. If a teacher was physically and verbally abusing my child, I'd take it very seriously indeed but no one ever really seemed to be too bothered by my distress.

The sense of loss and separation I once endured has been rendered obsolete since starting my own family but in terms of the relationship with my parents and brother, it is still there to an extent. There is a chasm, which allows no one across. I feel like a day member in a private club: accessing only the superficial areas and excluded from the inner sanctum. The situation is 'what it is'. Life is far too short to allow words to have more importance than time but many people miss this fact and allow too much time to pass. They also often say too much, assuming that the words can be 'un-said'. They can't. Name-calling and rows are one thing; threats are quite another. Tolerance is a word with limits: one's tolerance levels can be breached and love is no exception.

Now, having helped so many people and having had them divulge so many secrets and stories, while I fully understand that loving or nurturing your family members isn't obligatory, it's what parents should do as an instinctual response to the love they feel for their offspring; but it still alludes me as to why anyone would purposely take actions that they know will hurt someone but which they feel compelled to do anyway with blatant disregard, even when they know they are doing wrong. That takes a special kind of heart and thank heavens, my heart isn't built like that. Some people have tolerated huge loss, huge amounts of purposeful pain and anguish, but why? I don't get it.

I have always had a deep sense of connection to the outside world, probably because of the hyper-sensitisation of my nervous system due to the high-anxiety state, but I can't intellectualise the 'over the garden fence' mentality I experience every day, in which people believe that the superficial aspects of life are important and feel compelled to say and do things which maximise damage and embellish sadness.

I am constantly shocked as I watch people instigate aggressive exchanges and some people seem to enjoy conflict, enjoy being hurtful, threatening and vindictive.

Back to the UK again

I returned to the UK in September, and after a short stay at my parents' home I moved to Hull to start university, which on first inspection seemed acceptable ... just acceptable ... that was late summer but as the winter nights began to draw in, the picture changed considerably, trust me.

CHAPTER TWELVE

Hull and University, Dear God

I COMMENCED MY DEGREE in TV production at the University of Humberside in October. After five years living abroad the move to Hull from Worcestershire was quite a culture shock I can tell you, and even more so than the move from Heidelberg back to Kidderminster.

It was probably the unknown that I was more afraid of than anything else: the dark winter nights and not knowing anyone didn't help make me to settle in. I felt alone and scared, the first two weeks in Hull were dreadful. I saw and spoke to no one at all and sat alone in my flat watching TV until the first day of my first semester.

I loafed around Hull like a lost soul. The town was dull to say the least and the weather was cold and wet. I was used to a warmer climate and my Mallorcan tan made me stand out like a sore thumb. I felt alone, cold, bored and isolated, yet again, for the hundredth time in my life and I started to think about other people I knew and whether they had ever felt alone and isolated. Given that none of them had ever moved more than a few feet from where they were born, had never travelled alone, had not attended university and had not worked abroad, my conclusion was that they probably had no idea how it felt.

Isolation and loneliness are damaging. They open up the creative portals in the mind, they activate fear responses, they cause an avalanche of existentialist thoughts and they can happen even when people surround you.

Mental health issues develop when people are isolated. There are many well-documented cases of people developing severe and long-term mental illnesses and having experienced overwhelming loneliness, I can fully understand why.

What is worse is the sense that, even if you so wished, there would be nowhere to go, no one to call or visit. During some of my years with anxiety this is exactly how I felt. I believed that even if I had called a family member, none of them would have been able to say or do anything that could have changed how I felt; that's the loneliest feeling... to know people are there but not be able to reach out to them mentally.

It was such a relief to start my lectures, but the course was expensive. Textbooks, videotapes and field trips added up to much more than I could afford on my mature student's grant. I knew I was heading towards financial problems but what was I to do.

The course started well and my tutor was a very nice ex producer/director with lots of industry experience. As a mature student, I felt more in touch with him than with the other much younger students.

The students' behaviour was outrageous. The quantity of alcohol and drugs consumed made me wonder why they felt so confident that they would wake the next morning. A girl on the course tried her best over the first few weeks to get me drunk and also tried without a break to seduce me. Over the weeks her tops got tighter, her chat got dirtier and her subtle approach turned into frightening approaches that made me feel uncomfortable and anxious. I just didn't feel that way about her and she wasn't my 'type' at all.

Over the first few weeks, I began to settle in to student life but quickly realised that it wasn't for me and that I had made an enormous mistake. I couldn't bear being penniless and it was becoming increasingly apparent that if I wanted to continue, I was going to have to resign myself to being financially crippled or get a job.

I discussed my options with my tutor but he strongly advised me not to take on a part-time job, as the course would involve many field trips and lots of production work on locations outside of college time. I was stuck and I knew it but yet again, I couldn't back down. I knew that it would be perceived as failure, I knew I had nowhere else to go and I knew that if I didn't carry it through, I would be lost.

Financial constraints

A mature student's grant was, at the time, much less than a conventional student received and with no parental contribution, I knew this was going to prove more difficult than I could have ever imagined.

My brother was funded through university, even during holidays and the clear differences between his and my life became more evident. Whilst he was smoking, drinking, having Chinese takeaways and driving round in his Peugeot 205 GTI, I was staying home in order to buy video tapes.

A couple of my fellow students started to deal drugs to make a few pounds, while others saved for vital materials by eating canned dog food instead of more expensive human food – apparently when laced with ketchup and served with rice, it tasted dramatically better than most of the food available in the university refectory! One guy who lived on dog food looked ill. I'd like to say he had shiny hair or a wet nose but he didn't and as time passed his weight dropped and his attendance at university followed suit.

I made friends with a girl from London, Zoie, who had a really charming personality, albeit a little eccentric. We got on well and I started to realise that she felt a little more for me than I did for her so we decided to solve the problem by discussing how I felt. Man did this put me on the spot. While I found her physically attractive and she was a great friend, I didn't fancy her romantically. Our friendship was too good and she had a boyfriend in London who, after our discussion, promptly turned up on the scene.

On returning to the UK I had met a really lovely and pretty girl, a friend of my brother's, who turned up at my apartment in Hull one day. My brother had no idea that his friend had travelled for four hours to see me and at that time she had been dating another friend of mine. She wanted us to 'make a go of it' and wanted to move to Hull to be with me but it wasn't right and although I liked her very much, she returned home. I was saddened because she really was a great person but I had nothing to offer to a relationship at all, in fact, I knew that I would be a burden.

Burgled

Early in the semester we were told that we would be attending the Amsterdam Film Festival. On hearing the cost involved, I was worried to death, but a week later we boarded the ferry from Hull to Amsterdam. The journey was a nightmare. Nowhere to sleep, feeling nauseous as we wallowed left and right for what seemed like days. It was the most horrendous experience ever and as I did my best to retain composure, I wished that I had never returned to the UK at all.

On arriving in Amsterdam we discovered that the hostel had twin rooms and I had to share with a guy who appeared relatively normal but whose drug habit was legendary. Of course he was in his spiritual home as he knocked back hash cakes and weed like it was going out of fashion. Three days in Amsterdam dragged. The film festival was a farce. The films were dreadful, arty for arts sake and badly shot. It was boring and a complete waste of money and time.

I was looking forward to returning to Hull, which said something of the Amsterdam experience; I even found the red-light district boring.

Walking back to my apartment I opened the door and found ... nothing. Everything had gone. My TV, video recorder, video camera, and the thirty-five-millimetre camera my grandma had bought me for my twenty-first birthday, my clothes, all my videos, CDs and everything else the thieves managed to grab. They had ransacked my home, the only place I felt I could just *be* ... they had taken my possessions, some irreplaceable and Hull became instantaneously a thousands times worse than it had previously been to me.

I was so appalled. Nothing like that had ever happened to me before. All my years of travelling into every European country, of working in Germany, in fact in every aspect of my life up to that point had been free from such a selfish, cowardly and criminal act. What is wrong with people who do such malicious things to others? I don't think I'll ever understand what makes people like that tick.

The police told me there was nothing they could do. They said that none of the items would be retrieved and that the footprints they had found on my windowsill had been a child's.

The police sergeant told me that the kids who are convicted in Humberside are often sentenced to community service duties, the most accessed of which being a taxi from their home to the marina where they are forced to spend a day having sailing lessons. No wonder there's so much crime, there seems to be no justice system and certainly no fear of consequences that would prevent reoffending.

Hull became hell to me. I truly hated it. I felt trapped, vulnerable and so very pissed off that the course I chose had taken me to a horrendous place.

New relationships

Soon after the course started I'd met a girl from North Wales and we developed a relationship over the following few months. Gill suffered from Crohn's Disease, which meant that she had undergone major surgery that had left her with various health problems. As I discovered more about her illness, I switched to nurturing mode and at first this worked quite well, looking back now I suppose it made me feel needed.

She was a sweet girl with problems. She was pretty and interesting and made me laugh. She had periods of being completely well but could change quite quickly, especially after receiving vitamin B12 supplement injections once every month. As we got to know each other she became more relaxed around her true self and me soon became apparent. After a time, her own anxiety became very noticeable, she had an obsession about having contracted the HIV virus during her operation, after hearing a radio programme on the subject and from then on it was all I heard about. She also believed she had seen Elvis during the time she went through this trauma which worried me ... why Elvis? She was convinced she had died and been brought back by him, but whether there was any truth in this story remained a mystery.

My searching mind constantly flitted from subject to subject. One minute I'd be internalizing symptoms and thoughts about existentialism and my health, the next I'd be pondering my relative size in the universe and the meaning of it all. I tried to focus on my work but it was damn near impossible.

All through this period I was plagued by 'what ifs' – these focused mostly on health, sexuality, existence, religion, self-harming and others; they were constant, disturbing and overwhelming. Pure O is so misunderstood by psychology and medicine. No one could explain what caused it and the thousands of sufferers I have now helped all report that no professional has ever provided a satisfactory explanation. I now understand it fully and my reassurances have helped tens of thousands to stop fearing this symptom. There thoughts represent what is most unlikely NOT what is likely and to erase them is so simple when you know how. It's part of what we now do.

For some reason I couldn't get my diet right and I started suffering with chronic indigestion as my weight started to escalate.

Day and night Gill would fly into rages, pack and leave in the night, cry or go into some sort of trance where she would sit in her room and stare into space for hours, rocking from front to back, any attempt to attract her attention was ignored.

My brother witnessed one of these trance sessions while visiting me and couldn't understand why I endured it. The truth is I wanted to, I guess, I also needed someone to care about me and sometimes she offered that support as I sank deeper and deeper into chronic anxiety but mostly she focused on herself and her ever-increasing isolating selfishness.

I looked a complete mess by this time. I was heavier than I'd ever been and physically I looked weak and old. My hair was long, I'd stopped exercising and my diet was appallingly bad. I was also smoking at least twenty cigarettes a day, which I hated, but I believed it helped me to relax; they didn't, in fact, more often than not, they made my heart race. I hated the taste, the effect and the morning aftermath of smoking too many the night before.

The sergeant major

Nicotine is a stimulant and anyone who says that it calms them down is deluded, it's a physical impossibility: one cigarette produces the same effect as eating a tablespoon of sugar. While smoking doesn't always necessarily cause anxiety, it can help to perpetuate it. Like any ingested substance, nicotine has to be 'dealt with' by the body and as it metabolises the chemical, a myriad of physical changes happen as the body attempts to protect itself and maintain chemical equilibrium. So during anxiety recovery, smoking should be minimised but not eliminated (you don't need to add withdrawal to the mix). Of course, I didn't know that at the time so I went on smoking, the quantity escalating in line with my anxiety levels.

I was becoming tired, both physically and emotionally. My girlfriend's parents were absolutely no help at all, and her father, a rather pompous and overbearing military man, seemed to blame me for her problems. In return, I couldn't stand him so it was more a case of tolerance than respect.

He also seemed to be obsessed with his daughter, which was, at times, uncomfortable and a little creepy. Her mother was lovely but seemed wise to the situation and powerless to do anything. She was clearly much more intelligent than her husband and they were, to my mind, a complete mismatch and sometimes I detected that although he held a perceived position of authority within the family, she would respond to him with a what I believed to be ridicule. She was never disrespectful but I could tell he irritated her.

Although all of our friends saw what was happening and said that they worried about me constantly, I knew that a confrontation with her obsessive father was inevitable. I knew that whatever I said wouldn't 'wash' with him. Whatever she did to stress me, take advantage of me or undermine me, he either backed her up or didn't believe me.

My anxiety increased and quickly became constant and chronic. I felt dizzy, disorientated and unsteady and had started experiencing severe chest pains and shortness of breath. I had started to imagine that I was dying of horrific diseases, heart disease or cancer being the two most regular obsessions as well as AIDs. My anxiety-fuelled logic told me that if Gill had it then so did I! I obsessed about infection, illness and contamination. I washed every five minutes, I checked everything I touched and I hated the way she left mess wherever she went that I then had to touch.

Anxiety can take many forms, although this was never explained to me at the time and now, having helped tens of thousands of people with the same thoughts and obsessions, I know that they form part of the anxiety response and that they, like every other anxiety symptom, are easily curable. Obsessing about, well, everything in fact, is normal ... it may not *feel* normal, but it truly is because despite feeling like obsession the driving force behind the conscious experience of those thoughts are the risk assessments that the subconscious does in order to find *real* risk ... the risk assessment done when we are in real danger as part of the flight-or-fight response ... the emotion of fear.

You see, because the subconscious has no language, has no understanding of words and how we apply language to feelings, emotions, thoughts and experiences, when the brain sends out neural 'data' to assess a risk, our conscious mind registers it and applies language to it so that we can communicate how that neurological 'message' *feels*. Like describing hunger for example.

We use language to describe these 'notions' as obsessive thoughts, inappropriate thoughts or scary thoughts, but they are, in fact, none of these things, they are simply our mind's way of discovering risk.

'What if' thoughts are risk assessments. *What if I get ill? What if I die? What if I contract an infection? What if I don't flick the lights switch on eight times?* All risk assessments intended to assess and minimise true risk.

No matter how anxiety manifests – panic disorder, generalised anxiety disorder, OCD, Pure O, PTSD or an eating disorder – this mechanism is the cause. Forget the catalyst that gave rise to your first bout of anxiety, this core, human mechanism is to blame and nothing else.

Getting help

On returning home from university during the summer break, I decided to visit the family GP. He was very supportive and came to the conclusion that I was suffering from acute anxiety.

At twenty-four this information was difficult for me to digest, I guess I had more of an insight than most into the physiology of the human body, my mother was a nurse and I inherited her interest in medicine. I reluctantly accepted the doctor's diagnosis; I now know that this reluctance to accept diagnoses is a common feature of anxiety-related illnesses and part of the risk assessment process I just spoke of. *What if he got the diagnosis wrong? What if he is missing something and I die?*

I have always felt uneasy about taking any medication, which is perhaps a symptom of a lifelong underlying anxiety problem, but the doctor assured me that my symptoms would be fairly short lived if treated early. My prior experiences and the fact that I had never been completely anxiety free in my life told me otherwise, but at the time it was a case of taking the advice and having someone to turn to or continuing being alone with my suffering.

I just wanted to feel better and I wasn't concerned about how that was achieved. At twenty-four, pubs and girlfriends are far more appealing and mortality and awareness of physical weakness is, normally, a foreign notion. I wanted a 'quick fix' because I was tired and frustrated, scared and alone again.

My doctor decided that the best course of action would be to treat me medicinally with a tranquiliser that would prevent the symptoms from worsening and give me a little respite to make some life decisions that would alleviate some of my ever-increasing stress.

I agreed to take the medication and left feeling reassured that I had made the right decision and was, probably, on the road to feeling better.

Doctors have a massive responsibility. As general practitioners they have both a great deal of general medical knowledge and a responsibility to each of their patients, however, they also have to recognise that they don't know everything and allow those with greater knowledge to do their jobs and help those who truly know how to cure anxious people. They and they alone are responsible for correct and swift diagnosis of conditions that aren't always obvious. There are good doctors and there are bad doctors and I don't envy their job one bit. However, I do expect a person that has the power to make or break someone to be conscientious and honest enough to stay informed, to continue their research, training and education after leaving medical school, to look at holistic solutions. Not in the sense that most people would define holistic but in the sense that psychosomatic illness and medical practice exists, despite the naysayers and that the mind has *total* control over the body, which suggests with certainty that it can mend itself in most cases.

I am not denying that medication has its place, but not in the treatment of anxiety disorders. Why ingest chemicals? Is it curative? No. Is it useful? No! So why do they insist on doing it? Because many traditional medical practitioners don't understand the true nature of high-anxiety conditions, they don't have enough training to deal with them, they follow prescriptive guidelines that are based on chemistry rather than human biological truth and many don't have the time to listen to and truly *treat* their patients.

I know that what we do at The Linden Centre cures people, the evidence is stacked high since 1997. Thousands of people provide statements, from stay-at-home mums to celebrities and aristocracy. Many doctors, psychologists and clinics refer patients to us, but there are more that don't. Why? Why would anyone discourage or undermine what works when they *know* that what they do doesn't cure people? Why would anyone knowingly undermine our in-house qualified psychologists and psychotherapists?

'Specialists' either use 'treatments' knowing that they don't work or they don't know how to cure patients, either way both scenarios are unacceptable to me.

Life on medication

The tablets made me feel a little more able to cope initially. Their effect was short lived but they gave me enough time after taking the dose in the morning to assess and plan my day while feeling stoned off my face. Actually, all they were was addictive, high-inducing chemicals but for two hours, quite honestly, I didn't give a crap. Within two hours of taking the pill I would be back to the same old anxious me, there was no escape from how I was feeling and little did I know that the Diazepam was making things worse … far worse.

My mother assured me that she had taken Diazepam, Valium as it is commonly called, and that they were a great support in times of stress. This might be true if the doctors would only follow the manufacturers recommended dosage guidelines. Mum had given me hers at certain times during my teens but I don't honestly remember whether they helped. I don't think anything would have stopped the barrage of anxious thoughts.

The doctor gave me ninety tablets and I never actually received any dosage directions. They were always dispensed in a plastic bottle and not in a box with a leaflet. I now know what the leaflet says about dosages and safe, recommended periods of use. If I had known this information back then, things would have been very different believe me. It was the doctor's responsibility to inform me of the dangers of using a benzodiazepine or at very least for him to prescribe them using the manufacturers recommended guidelines, but he didn't. That's what his medical training taught him. They think that a few years in medical school allows doctors to diagnose and prescribe in this way. After all, would you get in a plane piloted by someone who got their pilot's licence the day before.

Consider the complexity of the human body, then consider the millions of environmental, dietary and social factors that could affect it, multiply the two and then multiply that number by the number of people on the planet – all with the same sophisticated physical and genetic makeup – and what you get is the most sophisticated machine known to man that can go wrong for a billion reasons and a doctor with a few of years' of training diagnosing and prescribing treatments who is ill-prepared to get it right every time.

Since 1997, we have helped hundreds of thousands of people and millions have accessed the anxiety-recovery resources, workshops, retreats and programs. My staff have spent tens of thousands of hours speaking to the people they cure. Specialists with a mountain of experience focused only on anxiety disorders and the cure.

Would you take your Lamborghini to a Fiat garage?

Within a few days of taking the Diazepam, I started to experience new symptoms like a racing heart, sweating and other disturbing and new sensations.

My anxiety was heightened legitimately this time. Chemically. My initial reaction was the thought that I was dying; that I was truly and seriously ill this time. I called the doctor's surgery and made an emergency appointment to visit him the same day. What a fool! Well two fools actually – the doctor and me.

His bedside manner was faultless, he sat and listened to my story and finally concluded that the dose he had recommended a few days' earlier was not enough and increased the dose by two tablets per day. He explained that, 'Someone of your size probably needs to take more for it to be effective.'

I went home reassured that the doctor, with all of his experience acquired over years of treating people with this medication and years of medical training, knew what he was doing and was doing the right thing for a twenty-four-year-old with anxiety.

Back to university life

The thought of returning to university and my girlfriend who was horrifying to be around, was truly terrifying but I knew what I had to do. After lengthy discussions with her, I was determined to find a solution to the stress I was experiencing, even if it meant radical action. The solution started with a phone call to my girlfriend's father.

She had an uncomfortable and somewhat strained relationship with her power crazed ex-military father. He doted on her completely and would never believe that she was capable of any wrong; the relationship was quite inappropriate at times. She manipulated him like a toy, but he thought she was as pure as driven snow. He was totally unsupportive and disregarded all of my attempts to help his daughter; he thought I was trying to upset their family or hurt his daughter. It couldn't have been further from the truth, but he made me the enemy.

I felt very concerned that she had started cutting classes, lying to our tutors and her parents, and that I was taking all of the responsibility. I started completing her course work for her and making excuses for her absence. She behaved like a child. She expected me to take over her father's role, to support her, to carry her when she needed it, to dote on her, to make it 'all go away' for her. Not only did I not feel well enough to give her that level of support but also why should I? I had only just met her and she was bringing me down lower than I had ever been before. Despite being chronically agoraphobic, I forced myself to go to university every day, to drive and to act normally; the panic attacks were the inevitable result every time but she didn't care and I didn't have a choice.

I went to bed that night but couldn't sleep, primarily because of the constant crying from my girlfriend, but also because of the distinct smothering sensation and the feeling that my eyes were staring even when they were closed. I was becoming very, very scared by my symptoms but also by the overwhelming reality of the prison I was in. I also noticed that I had started to get prickly spikes of hair all over the top of my head, which told me that my hair was falling out; was this due to stress or the inevitability of genetic baldness?

I persevered for a few more days but I experienced new sensations every day, and every day they grew more intense, more frightening and more obscure. The smothering sensation became worse, now I really couldn't get my breath and the right side of my face went numb and felt like it was drooping. My eye would water and sometimes I would dribble out of the side of my mouth. My left arm felt heavy again and my neck, shoulders and back felt very painful.

Now I was convinced I had a brain tumour or had had a stroke, what else could it be? I returned to my doctor a few days later. By now I had the distinct feeling that I really was not coping, that I was losing my mind and I truly felt, for the first time in my life, like I should be in a mental facility. My mind was out of control. I couldn't decipher what was real and what wasn't. My subconscious and my body were acting independently of my conscious will and the resulting sensations and thoughts made me feel like I was living outside of myself that my consciousness existed outside of my physical body. I never knew it was possible to feel this way. How were my body and mind able to create such an illusion?

The doctor was convinced I was suffering from anxiety and his objective and educated recommendation, was to increase my dose of Diazepam. He added that it would be acceptable for me to nibble a quarter tablet 'when and if' I needed it. I was so relieved. I definitely felt calmer after taking my tablet, the doctor assured me that the time in which I felt so ill in between doses would get shorter and shorter; I accepted the advice and returned home ... what a mistake!

I had started to stay at home more, I felt at risk when leaving the house, and when I did venture out, it was never alone. I couldn't place the fear, it wasn't attached to anything really, and it just escalated quickly when I moved further and further from my front door. I felt weak and stupid and that people had started to laugh at me. No one could understand why I was behaving that way, most of all me.

Agoraphobia

Agoraphobia is an extension of the risk mitigation created by the anxiety response as we retreat from danger during flight-or-fight but to a sufferer it *feels* like fear, it feels like there is true risk present and it feels like it will never end. I know this now.

Sufferers make the assumption that an anxiety disorder has something to do with mental health, that it is a true representation and reaction to our environment. However, the truth is, it is false fear. Every symptom and thought experienced is activated by the emotion of fear, emotions aren't illnesses ... they're emotions! They're controllable, regulated human responses to external data and anyone who suggests they can't be re-calibrated and stopped is talking complete rubbish. Don't listen to them.

I had started getting burning pains in my chest and this only reinforced my theory that I was physically and gravely ill. I had almost completely withdrawn from my social life at university, my tutor had noticed that I wasn't behaving 'normally' and he called me to his study in order to identify the core issues and offer his help.

I was reluctant to talk to him about my problem, after all he would be grading my term papers and I thought that it might affect my course work. I did confess to him that I wasn't feeling well and told him about the problems that my girlfriend was experiencing. He knew she was unwell and admitted to knowing the about the pressure she was putting me under. Some of my course-mates had been to see him, concerned that I was looking unwell.

He was very understanding and suggested that we meet regularly so that he could support me and ensure that my grades were not affected by my anxiety, my girlfriend or the fact that I was carrying the burden of much of her course work. I was so relieved to gain his support and understanding.

By now my symptoms were becoming much more acute and I had started to experience very real episodes of extreme anxiety, which were much more intense and developed very much faster than the daily, generalised anxiety. At the time I was scared and unsure of what was happening to me. I thought I was experiencing symptoms of heart problems, which fuelled the anxiety even more.

The pains in my chest were getting worse. Coupled with the smothering sensations and the numbness in my face I was becoming more and more convinced that whatever this illness was, it was escalating quickly and that its source would be discovered only after it had killed me. It felt so real, so 'cellular' as if every cell in my body was conspiring against me.

I decided to make an appointment to see the doctor about the pains. I really feared the worst. My father had had a double heart bypass at the age of forty-two, so it was not unimaginable that I could have a heart problem too. The doctor knew of my father's illness and was concerned when I described my symptoms; the look of concern on her face also served to massively fuel my fears.

Doctors are so responsible but sometimes so irresponsible. It's the absence of knowledge that expedites and adds to suffering when an anxious person consults a doctor that may, not only, have no idea what to say but also no idea how to say it to a sufferer in order to prevent more fear from developing.

My dad's heart problems underlined the fact that, because of the direct genetic link, I could be heading towards the same problems. My fear was growing, I could feel it multiplying, unfolding inside of me and the more I focused on it or was aware of it, the faster it grew. In my heart, I knew I was ill and like all sufferers, all I needed was a constant stream of reassurance. Reassurance that would satisfy my need for a short time but would, as always, return later or turn its attention to another symptom or obsession. That's the true nature of an anxiety disorder: when one fear is 'capped' another opens.

The doctor suggested that I go to the local hospital for some tests. As the words left her mouth, I felt the blood drain from my face, my heart started to race, the smothering sensation got worse, I started to sweat and (I thought I) knew then that I was a dying man. It was like turning on a tap, the anxiety welled up and crashed over me like a tsunami. This was, to date, the worst of many full-blown and intense panic attacks I had experienced.

The doctor arranged for an emergency appointment but I still had to wait about a week, which was painful as I waited to find out whether or not I was about to die. At my appointment I had chest x-rays. A few more insufferable days ensued until I received the test results, which were, of course, negative.

The doctor concluded that I was suffering from chronic indigestion, a common symptom of anxiety. This fact wasn't mentioned to me at the time of the original consultation but days later when the fear had really established itself in my psyche after my anxiety levels had had time to increase even more. The doctor prescribed an antacid to treat the indigestion which helped for a while but the pain wasn't just indigestion, it felt like muscle pain and now I know that, this too, is a common and expected symptom of high anxiety.

There was something wrong, I knew it deep inside, at least that's how real it felt, and I was getting worse by the day. My girlfriend was a living nightmare; her insistence that she was dying of AIDs was becoming an obsession for both of us. Day or night she would scream and shout totally unprovoked, waking me and causing me to feel terrified as I scrambled to attend to her at all hours. Then she'd pack her bags and walk out. I would find myself chasing down the road after her in my boxer shorts, trying to apply reason to her insane behaviour. Sometimes this would happen at 4 a.m., and then I'd end up having a full-blown panic attack while she slept soundly having left a trail of destruction in her wake.

Over the next months we both became almost reclusive, leaving the house rarely, only to buy food and in my case to attempt attending university, an activity that my girlfriend had almost totally given up. My symptoms changed daily, the list was almost endless and was becoming increasingly more difficult to cope with.

Derealisation and depersonalisation

I had always suffered from derealisation and depersonalisation in waves as my anxiety levels ebbed and flowed. Derealisation was manageable – that sense of dreaminess, removal from reality, of living through a frosted glass screen.

Depersonalisation was harder to manage and to come to terms with. Sometimes I'd wake in the night and not know who I was or sometimes I'd see myself from outside myself as if my *doppelganger* was examining me. Both are the weirdest sensations but both are harmless, anxiety related and curable.

I've heard people with derealisation disorder and depersonalisation disorders talk about themselves as if they are separate from the anxiety, as if they require different treatment. I'm afraid I don't agree. Many of the people I have helped developed these symptoms after taking drugs and believe that they have done irreparable damage to their brains. Depersonalisation (DP) and Derealisation (DR) are nothing more than the manifestation of small changes made in the brain in an attempt to protect it during the flight-or-fight response. Rather like the leather 'blinkers' put on plough horses in order to keep them straight and focused on what is ahead, DP and DR are chemical 'blinkering' which focus the person on the true threat during fight or flight. These can both be dealt with incredibly quickly when you know what they are and what to do about them but when they develop, it's easy to allow them to dominate your life and become your anxious focus.

Both DP and DR can become immediately apparent after taking drugs, and cannabis is the most common culprit. But again, these can both be erased quickly when you know how.

At the time, however, I thought I was losing my mind and my irrational thoughts were fuelling this belief.

I had started to get thoughts associated with and focusing on death, and these quickly became an obsession that stayed with me constantly. I just couldn't shake them and they were there when I woke in the morning; and still there at night as I lay in bed focusing on how I was feeling. These thoughts were disturbing but not as frightening as what was to come.

It started very gradually, at first I would ignore it, dismissing it as stupid and irrational thoughts but as it became worse I became very concerned. I started imagining all sorts of aggressive and sexual encounters with people I would meet. Family members, fellow students and complete strangers were the subject of these horrendous scenarios. I would be holding a conversation with someone while picturing them in sexual or aggressive clinches with me.

I would picture myself hitting them violently or performing a sexual act with them, more disturbingly, these thoughts were not gender specific and as a heterosexual this was very disturbing.

I would stand next to people I knew, love and respect and imagine myself, in my mind's eye performing an inappropriate sexual act.

When I walked past a knife in the kitchen, I would imagine myself stabbing someone, or myself, with it and even an open window would induce fantasies of throwing someone out of it or seeing someone hanging through the glass cut to shreds in my mind's eye.

It was after enduring these thoughts for a number of weeks that I decided to see a psychologist and got a referral from my doctor to do so.

Despite not having a clue what they were caused by or why my brain was manifesting such thoughts, my psychologist assured me that he had treated other patients with all of my thoughts and symptoms. This went some of the way to reassuring me that I was not going crazy but without a clear understanding of what they were, I was still worried that everyone was missing a diagnosis of psychosis or worse.

Understanding Pure O

I now know what these thoughts are, how they are caused and what they mean. They are commonly referred to as Pure O, which, yet again, suggests a separate condition and most suffers do believe that they have developed a condition called Pure O. They are all too aware that they also might suffer from anxiety; maybe panic attacks, OCD, agoraphobia and a variety of other symptoms.

Medicine and psychology treat all these disorders as separate conditions but they are all, without exception, caused by one mechanism in the brain – fear. They are simply a variety of physical and mental manifestations of the responses that are normal, natural and expected during high anxiety and the flight or fight response.

You see, because anxiety is a transient emotion and part of our safety system, once activated, it should be used and deactivated, normally within minutes when a real threat is present, say during an accident or when attacked for example.

In anxiety disorders when the anxiety response is perpetuated, the symptoms, which would normally disappear quickly, are also perpetuated causing aches and strains, sensations and thoughts that normally wouldn't have time to develop.

Every single symptom experienced during an anxiety disorder is normal, expected and harmless.

These Pure O thoughts are simply manifestations of the 'what if' risk assessment 'notion' sent out during high anxiety, so despite *you* consciously putting language to the 'notion' by making '**what if** I killed my mum' mean 'I want to kill my mum', the truth is that what your mind is actually trying to understand, without language, in the form of neural questioning designed to get an answer from your sensory organs (eyes, ears, mouth, nose, skin), is 'what is the worst possible thing I could do to this person in this current situation?'

Do you see the difference? It's a risk assessment. It's not that you'd *actually do* those things. All your mind is trying to do is keep *you* safe by asking, 'What if *I did?*'

Indeed, more importantly, these thoughts represent the action you would never take, rather than what is likely; a risk assessment wouldn't be productive if the perceived outcome were positive. I have helped many people with these thoughts and, for the sake of demonstrating how these thoughts work: homosexuals will imagine having heterosexual encounters in the same way as heterosexuals will imagine homosexual encounters in their risk assessments.

Millions of people worldwide have fallen prey to these thoughts, believing they are going crazy. Millions of health professionals world over have no idea what these thoughts are. Over the last sixteen years, we have reassured tens of thousands of people and my videos about Pure O have been watched on YouTube and elsewhere tens of thousands of times by people desperate to discover what's wrong with them.

Never in twenty-seven years was one single healthcare professional able to explain what they were and never has one of our clients reported to us that they have had clear explanations from theirs.

Getting counselling

I embarked on a weekly counselling session, which I had to pay for out of my student grant. I got a student loan, which helped, but my course was not cheap and I found myself getting deeper into an economic pit.

Over the following months I didn't improve, my doctor prescribed a drug called Stelazine to knock the edge off my anxiety. Stelazine is an anti-psychotic, but, in small doses, is prescribed to calm anxiety symptoms. It was completely ineffectual of course, except for making me drowsy and irritable and causing me to experience a horrible buzzing sensation as if a bee was flying around in my head. I perceived this as a constant, fast vibration not as a noise.

When the doctor realised I was not responding to the Diazepam any more, he decided I should take it as required, and I did. I think that at one stage I was taking six to eight tablets per day until I was taking 30–80 mg per day.

I increased my dosage as needed, but my list of symptoms and sensations increased too, and I was beginning to think that life was unbearable. I felt so alone and no one was capable of saying the right thing to me. I just wanted someone to tell me what was going on in my body and mind – not reassurance, FACTS. No psycho-babble, no analysis, no blaming, just simple, scientific fact that explained the symptoms and thoughts. No one was able to provide an explanation.

I was too scared to live and too scared to die ... what I call 'the anxiety sufferer's mantra'.

I was becoming more and more agoraphobic, I did not want to leave home at all and when I did manage to get past the front door, I felt worse, much, much worse. It was unbearable. I felt that I couldn't drive anywhere alone and just going to the corner shop only twenty yards from home filled me with dread and resulted, more often than not, in a panic attack and hours of terror.

The psychologists and doctors could explain some of my symptoms by reading textbooks descriptions of physiological changes that occur through anxiety; but they couldn't explain everything I was experiencing and that worried me. How could they not understand fear, anxiety and human emotion, why did what they told me make so little sense?

I, as many anxiety sufferers have described to me since, was sick to the back teeth of hearing about the 'flight-or-fight' response and changing my thoughts to change how I feel. I was sick of having CBT-based nonsense shoved down my throat, mostly by well-meaning counsellors, but also by some who, through desperation, to pay their bills, chose to mislead and mistreat me as they do with most suffers under the guise of 'there is no cure, only management'.

Do I sound angry? Well I am. CBT has its place but, in my opinion, relapse prevention programme crash and burn is useless in recovery from high-anxiety conditions. No, not just useless, but also, potentially, damaging and any psychologist worth their salt knows it but chooses to ignore it. CBT used to treat anxiety disorders isn't based on psychological, medical or scientific understanding; it's based on fee building.

Let me explain … You see, in a nutshell, CBT makes the assumption that conscious thought precedes the emotional/physical response: we see a man with a gun, we think, *Oh a man with a gun, what shall I do? I know I'll attack him.* The thought and decision-making is conscious and precedes the activation of the flight-or-fight response: the emotion of fear. What utter nonsense. What utterly flawed and dangerous science. This flawed science perpetuates anxiety disorders in millions of people around the world.

I developed what presented like some sort of urinary tract infection, which included genital itching, pain and burning which, yet again, set off my anxiety. The doctor sent me for tests once again but they came back negative, as you would probably expect by now. I later discovered that this would go away when I ceased taking Diazepam but at the time no one asked me what medication I was taking or thought to question what else might be causing these symptoms.

The coward

I struggled on for nearly two years, but my life was not getting any easier. Although Gill and I were still living together I was growing more distant psychologically from her. Instead of the nurturing feelings I once had for her, she now made me feel sad and angry, I just wanted to leave.

I realised that if I could just make it to the summer holidays I could take advantage of the inevitable separation by returning to Worcestershire.

It was a cowardly way to finish a relationship but I was not feeling well enough to cope with the turmoil of a drawn-out break-up and the thought of her father coming to Hull and a confrontation developing, filled me with dread. I didn't want a negotiation; I just wanted it all to stop.

She still failed to see sense, she became ever more obsessive, she looked ill and I felt truly sad and distressed for her, but she and her father had made my life a misery for nearly two years and a break up was inevitable and the right solution. The childishness from both parties was simply intolerable.

I waited out the remainder of the semester and we parted on friendly terms vowing to visit each other throughout the summer. I had no intention of doing so, but her father made it quite clear that anything that would upset his daughter would be quite unacceptable. I feared the potential confrontation, not him, he didn't scare me at all but the discomfort he could create was not something I could have coped with at the time.

I was finding it difficult to walk let alone become involved in a fight, so I just stood and watched as he cleared out her possessions. The last straw came when they took my VCR with them. She claimed that she had paid for it but she didn't even pay rent. I wasn't prepared to argue. She had sold some of her possessions, even her father's expensive Canon camera to buy cigarettes and alcohol. She deceived him constantly and despite their strange relationship, didn't seem to even like him very much, but he still doted on her.

As the car disappeared down the road I was relieved but alone. I slowly packed up the clothes I would need for the summer, locked up the house and returned to Worcestershire. The journey home was probably the most difficult trip I have ever made, I was alone, far from home and I felt very, very unwell.

CHAPTER THIRTEEN

Retreat from Hull and Meeting Beth

I JUST DIDN'T FEEL very welcome at my family home – with emphasis on the word *feel* because at the time I didn't have an accurate 'read' on what I felt. I suppose they had got used to me living away and I guess I was the invader in the 'new, revised' family unit. I felt alienated and unwanted. This isn't to say that *was* how my family felt but in the depths of my anxiety it seemed to be the case.

I do know that they didn't understand how I felt. I tried and tried to explain, but they were simply unequipped to understand. There are only two groups of people who are qualified to understand, explain and advise on anxiety matters: those who are going through it and those who have been through it. I get that now.

As I said earlier, I used to feel – despite trying my best to vocalise the experience of the sensations, thoughts and symptoms – as if I was speaking a foreign language and the exercise was frustrating and very isolating.

Of course doctors, psychiatrists and psychologists can communicate anecdotal evidence, research, developed treatments and reassurance, but unless they belong, or belonged to, one of the two groups I mentioned above they are really not at all qualified to understand anxiety suffering, the symptoms, their thoughts or the sufferer themselves.

My mother had experienced a bout of anxiety after my grandfather died but, for whatever reason, her life circumstances conspired to produce a recovery and she admits that in comparison, her disorder was mild and short lived. To my knowledge she never experienced anything like it again. But even she failed to understand my condition, which I found difficult. I just felt totally alone.

I fought with my parents continually, the more I asked for help the angrier they became. Eventually this became a vicious cycle, the more I asked for help the more they ignored me, the more they ignored me the more I fought for recognition and help.

I can understand their frustration at not being able to stop what I was going through but sometimes all it takes is patience, kindness and a hug; and actually, I think, that was all I wanted from them. I can't blame them for their inability to nurture me at the level I required back then, we are all products of our own experiences and environments and I guess that because they didn't have personal experience of the condition, it was outside of their range of understanding. Since then I've met thousands of anxious people who feel the same way.

At this point in time I was taking between 40–90 mg of Diazepam, Stelazine and Prozac every day, each tablet designed to cancel out the symptoms, which I later found out, were being caused by the others. I lasted out the summer, day by day, on the edge of my nerves and literally too scared to live and too scared to die.

I made the decision that returning to Hull would have been a ridiculous and counterproductive exercise at least, so I applied to Wolverhampton University to finish my degree there.

Wolverhampton is only 13 miles from my hometown and the course was fairly similar to the one in Hull. After all I had endured in Hull for two years, I was loath to throw away my chance of graduating. Wolverhampton University accepted me soon after. What a relief it was.

I decided to try and work during the summer – industry-related work that would serve to bolster my CV and give me the much-needed financial boost to continue my studies. I wasn't really fit to work, but I think I was beginning to believe that 'I'm damned if I do and damned if I don't'. I couldn't feel much worse so what had I got to lose? To an extent, I have always had that philosophy about every aspect of my life. I am not a quitter!

Work experience and Beth

I contacted a local TV company and managed to land some work experience. The studio was just down the road from home and I could just about manage to drive there without losing control or the smothering sensations getting out of control.

I started work a week later and was pleased to see that my boss, Beth, was pretty and funny. We hit it off straight away and soon became close friends. Our friendship gradually developed into a relationship, but Beth had been in a very strained long-term relationship, which she insisted was dead. She knew nothing about my condition and I orchestrated my life and our joint activities with such skill so that she had no idea what lurked beneath the surface.

She broke up with her partner after some pretty intense emotional encounters, but she felt guilty and returned to him a month later on 23rd December.

I was devastated of course, but decided to take my mum's advice and back off and give her time to decide what she really wanted. I did this reluctantly, believing that I had lost her forever. One month later she left him for good and things were perfect again.

She knew I had some health issues by now. The subject needed to be broached so we sat down together and I told her everything. She was wonderful, she understood and sympathised but I am sure she had no idea what could and did eventually happen.

We established a very solid relationship quite quickly; a medium had told her that she would be my guardian angel. It appears that she was correct. In the meantime, of course, my anxiety fuelled doubts and fears but the distraction of being in a new relationship and the fun we were having was enough to subdue the extreme panic perhaps.

I couldn't have wished for a more supportive partner, it would have been so easy for her to walk away, but she stayed and supported me. To this day, I don't know what I would have done without her. As time progressed and life was becoming more enjoyable, I started to believe that the remainder of my symptoms could be attributed to the cocktail of drugs I was still consuming. They weren't. They were still the anxiety but I had to 'hang my hat on something' in order to intellectualise what I was experiencing.

Starting out together

Things seemed to be looking: I was making a little money doing some fairly restricted TV work and Beth and I had decided to buy a place together. After a short search, we found a two-bedroom apartment in a converted country club in a small nearby town on the River Severn. The apartment was light and airy with high ceilings and windows to match and was perfect for us.

I still couldn't travel too far from home and felt really very ill most of the time, but it was more manageable. This was due more to my self-reassurance that I wouldn't die rather than an improvement in my general health. The most disturbing symptoms were impotence, urinary tract infections, paralysis, rashes, diarrhoea and tinnitus. I was accustomed to panic attacks and derealisation being regular part of my day while depersonalisation fluctuated between being a light fog and peasouper.

Pure O, the sexual, homosexual, aggressive and existentialist thoughts, also fluctuated but were ever present, usually when I met with family and friends. I had always had them but they escalated in my twenties and were pretty much constant at this point, which was a constant source of fear as I am gentle and heterosexual by nature. Beth and our gay friends now joke that I am the gayest straight man they know, which is odd but as they say, it's only about the shaved head and my love of clothes and fashion.

The other symptoms were what I would call classic anxiety symptoms and as such, I could reliably dismiss them.

I was having regular physiotherapy because of the back problem due to fracturing my coccyx in school, a tale I related earlier in the book, and tension, which caused neck and shoulder pain. The counsellors came and went but not one of them could give me a single, logical explanation for my symptoms, let alone reassurance, or provide any helpful curative advice. No structure, no process, no hope.

I tried a faith healer – what a complete charlatan – hypnosis, CBT, NLP, a whole host of other talking therapies, I had allergy tests, I meditated ... Did any of it help? No, not even slightly.

I was also referred to a psychiatrist at the local hospital, a surly, old and unfriendly man with grey skin that seemed to match his hair, clothes, office and personality. He sat, legs crossed, folder on knee, listening to me as I told my story for, what felt like, the millionth time. His advice was legendary: buy pornography, go home and 'w**k' and 'do so until you feel better'.

No comment, but I had the feeling I wasn't the one that needed 'relief', but he did deserve relieving of his job for his useless, and offensive, advice.

False hope was around every corner for me but no one ever said to me that a cure was possible: without exception, they tried to teach me to manage my anxiety; to learn to live with it using coping strategies but I knew that there *must be* a cure out there. But at the time I could help thinking, surely I am not the only person who ever suffered from this 'mysterious' condition ... or perhaps I am!

The new doctor and getting drug-free

A new trainee doctor, Dr Claire Bolton, had started at my local surgery, and I decided to book an appointment with her – in the hope that a newly qualified doctor might have a fresh insight into newest therapies and drugs available. I was sick of seeing older doctors, mostly men, who had that 'holier than thou' attitude based purely on their age but not their medical efficacy.

I was right. Here initial reaction was one of complete horror. First, that any doctor could keep me on Diazepam for so long; and second that a generally healthy person could be so side tracked by a course of very severely misjudged decisions from a wide range of healthcare professionals.

During this time, Beth and I decided to move house too. We were too geographically removed from anything interesting, and I felt isolated when Beth was at work. This was mostly because I had I become so unwell again. I couldn't stand up without having a panic attack and travelling had almost become impossible.

Dr Claire reduced the Diazepam dose followed by the Stelazine. I was not misled by any promises of a symptom-free withdrawal program, as she advised me of what could happen as the Diazepam was reduced, and she was not wrong. However, I felt incredibly positive about this new regime, about my decision, but also incredibly scared of what could happen.

The first day on the reduced dose I felt marginally better, not well but just different somehow. The dose reduction was enough to make a difference as the synapses in my brain started to fire differently as the active drug was removed.

I now know that what I call 'seesawing' your dose, (not maintaining a regular dose), actually has a profound effect on its therapeutic power and doesn't allow your body to become accustomed to a regular and even dosage, which can have a very severe affect on how you feel, as it confuses your nervous system. Add to this seesawing effect, the fact that other physiological factors are dependent on the individual's chemical makeup so it is difficult to predict how this will make you feel and how difficult it will be to withdraw from it.

The second day I felt very anxious indeed. I woke in the morning with the familiar shaking feelings accompanied by a feeling and thoughts of morbid doom. But by this time I was so acclimatised to feeling unwell that these were simply another set of symptoms to tolerate, as I had tolerated them throughout my life. I had experienced these feelings before and although I didn't want them to return, they didn't scare me as much as before.

Looking back, I can remember how it felt and I am so glad that I no longer have to tolerate that overwhelming sense of doom. I sympathise with you and every sufferer but I also reassure you with all my heart that all of what you experience is transient no matter how it makes you feel or how long you have suffered.

Resigning yourself to the presence of the symptoms is actually an important element of recovery; it isn't giving up, but simply allowing something over which you have no power to happen, after all they are only sensations created by your subconscious mind and not the features of real illness. They may be highly unpleasant sensations but the more you give them credibility the more you empower them and perpetuate their existence. They are not harmful in any way and are simply the side effects of the anxiety response.

After about two weeks I decided it was time to reduce my tablets again. I decided on a four-week reduction period and that I would reduce my dose by 0.5 mg on each dose. This reduction doesn't sound much but its effect was profound.

I became much more anxious – but at least I knew why. I started experiencing what is called 'rebound anxiety', which in effect is like putting a cork in a bottle, shaking it up for years and then popping the cork. My brain and body came alive with a burst of confused nerve impulses.

The thoughts and sensations were extreme. From one moment to the next, I did not know how I would feel. The smothering sensations came back, but far worse than before. I felt like someone had their hands around my throat, choking the life out of me, and when I ate, I could feel a large lump in my throat that gave me the distinct feeling that I would choke. I shook visibly and when I walked forwards I felt as if an invisible hand was pushing me back by my forehead. Tingling, shaking, quivering, numbness, dizziness, and emotional turmoil: it was like being in a huge washing machine with items flashing past me. Momentarily I would recognise something as it became apparent and then in a flash it was gone again and replaced by something else.

I would sit, for hours sometimes, running my fingers through my hair, the feeling of which, at least, gave me the feeling that I was alive in my head. I felt as if my brain was slowly giving up, like I was slipping away. I know now that this is common in anxiety and withdrawal and is just the product of more confused nerve impulses.

I would tighten belts around my waste and wear tighter clothes just to feel like I was 'holding myself together'. I would often rub my thigh with increasing pressure in order to receive recognisable feelings from my body. I would stand, often for hours, at the basin in our bathroom, splashing my face with water and holding on to the porcelain with white knuckled hands.

No one can imagine the terror of anxiety unless they have lived it.

I called the doctor or the primary care centre at the local hospital day and night. They must have got so fed up with me calling, begging for help. I felt so stupid but my desperation drove me on. Consciously I knew I was being irrational but I couldn't stop myself. I felt like a silly child hidden in the body of an adult man and despite the shame, I continued.

I remember standing at the upstairs window of our house in the early hours of the morning, holding on to the window frame – if I had let go I would have collapsed – while on the phone to the primary care centre begging them for help. They never allowed me to visit them. I turned up there once, without calling first and they sent me away.

I felt like a leper, no one seemed to want to help me and people's reaction to me in general became devoid of any emotion or caring and that was only *if* they came anywhere near me.

Beth

During this time, I used to phone Beth at work, sometimes ten or more times a day, and I knew I was driving her mad. I was scared of losing her but I kept doing the things that were driving her away from me. I was powerless.

I was experiencing more extreme depersonalisation and derealisation, and sometimes I didn't even recognise myself when I looked in the mirror. I would stand for minutes staring at myself, knowing my name, my story and my family but not recognizing the face that stared back at me.

Beth would leave for work at 8 a.m. and work till 6 p.m., sometimes later. At lunchtime, she would sometimes make the twenty-two-mile round trip to help me to the toilet. I would sit and count the minutes till she came back. Wrapped in my duvet, huddled by the radiator, I tried to watch TV but it was impossible. My eyes wouldn't focus, I felt like I couldn't breathe, I couldn't eat and standing inevitably led to a panic attack caused by the belief that I would die if I moved. My chest felt like it was being crushed by a steel band and when I attempted to move, even shift my position, my heart would jump and race. Sometimes Beth wouldn't be able to get back to me at lunchtime and only the absolute fear that I would pee myself would make me shuffle down the corridor to the bathroom, as my anxiety escalated, peeing and panicking simultaneously.

On a couple of occasions I didn't make it and I had to clean the carpet and myself before Beth came back.

The shame was overwhelming. The sense of what I had become was consuming me and I had no idea what to do next. This wasn't 'me' it was a shadow of the person I could be.

It often felt as if my nasal passages were the size of a train tunnel; when I breathed it felt like I had no control over my breath, like my nose was a huge void in my head. I also had the distinct sensation that my mind had somehow left my head and was floating in front of my forehead, my head felt numb as if I was only alive in my eyes, which burned and became very sensitive to light. My left arm felt heavy again and my consciousness was constantly drawn to the numbness down the side of my face and head.

I tried to describe these feelings to my 'carers' but did they know how to respond? No, never. I would say that I felt that I was only living through my subconscious mind, that my body only kept on working because my subconscious mind maintained it and that all conscious thought was slowly slipping away. I thought that the explanation was clear but still no one understood.

At night I would lie awake staring into space. Even when my eyes were closed, I felt as if I was staring with my eyes wide, propped open. What a horrific sensation, and what was causing it? Fear, pure, high level fear. But of what? Actually of nothing tangible, just of the fear and the sensations and thoughts it caused.

I would fall asleep and wake screaming or throw myself across the room as if someone had pushed me. Beth was an angel for tolerating me, as I think most people would have thrown me out but she held me and reassured me night after night. I felt so ridiculous but the fear was so real.

I would crawl to the bathroom, the pain and restriction in my chest was unbearable, I thought it was my heart giving up.

During the day I would be at home alone, no visitors, they all kept away. It was amazing that none of my family even asked me how I was feeling. They never wanted to see me or talk to me on the telephone when I was feeling ill but during my moments of improvement they would ask for my help and support if they needed to have something lifted from the attic, collected, designed or built.

I began to feel as if they only wanted the healthy me and then only when they needed something from me. This fuelled my notion that I was alone in the world and only served to make me sadder and more anxious.

I think it's human nature to protect yourself from discomfort and pain and, in hindsight, I guess they were just protecting themselves from me. I was a thorn in everyone's side at the time. I knew I was being childish, dependent and illogical much of the time.

Nana Kay would sit with me if I could make it to her house. She looked after me. She was my best friend when I needed someone to support or reassure me, and she was one of life's true carers. She had a funny attitude to some things and could be venomous and outspoken when she needed to be, but she cared so much for me when I needed her most.

She would buy me chocolate when I felt weak and make me tea and scones with jam and meals when I needed them. I don't know what I would have done without her looking after me as I lay wallowing in my anxious thoughts on her sofa watching *Wheel of Fortune* or *Countdown*.

We had a pact that *if* she were able to contact me after she died, she would say the word 'Countdown', so that I knew she was with me. If anyone could break through the boundary between life and death it would be nana Kay, she was such a strong character and even when she became infirm and fed up with being frail, she stock-piled paracetamol so that she could take her own life. I admit I foiled the plan when I found them in the side pocket of her handbag. She was a tough old bird but was never ill during her life and died age ninety-four having told my mum that she wanted to have a stroke and die, which is exactly what she did a day later.

I was away on holiday when she finally passed away but I think she planned it that way ... I'll never know I guess, unless I mysteriously hear the word 'Countdown' whispered into my ear one day.

Nana P would also help me as much as she possibly could. She would sometimes collect me and take me to my hospital or psychologist appointments. Jan would always be with her and often we would stop for a drink somewhere or visit an antique shop. They were both amazing friends to me during my anxiety and when nana P died, I felt an even bigger hole appear in my life.

Both my beloved nanas died after my anxiety recovery, which was a true blessing and I was also blessed to have had them as grandparents, despite their eccentricities. I miss them every day.

Psychobabble

I started to see a gestalt psychotherapist that mum knew through work. She seemed nice at first but over the weeks she became quite tough. She would try and draw information out of me and sometimes I was confused as to whether the memories she dragged from my mind where real or not.

I remember driving home after one session in which she had tried to pull memories of conflict with my family out of me. I cried through, pretty much, the entire session and when I left, she had worked me into a frenzy about my parents. I remember wanting to grab the steering wheel and plough the car into a tree. I didn't know whether to confront my parents or kill myself. The pain was so raw and I felt so inappropriately and uncharacteristically aggressive. The next day I woke to find that the rage had subsided and so had the memories. I couldn't work with her any more. In total I had at least fifteen sessions at a great cost but I was more anxious at the end of it than I'd ever been before.

I experienced some pretty scary feelings and symptoms during this period; things that would make a well person question their sanity; experiences that can only usually be activated through alcohol or recreational drugs.

An example of one of these occasions was when I sat and watched a Welsh dragon fly around the living room. Did I dream it or was I hallucinating, I never found out. It seemed so real and I still remember how it looked as it dipped and curled around the furniture and hissed at me as it passed overhead.

I sat on the floor in the lounge wrapped in a blanket watching TV day in and day out for weeks. I couldn't sit on the sofa; it felt uncomfortable and hot on my body. I experienced temperature fluctuations all of the time, and I would be sweating one minute and cold and shivering the next.

My ribs ached all day and night as if I had been kicked and bruised. I developed severe pains in my hands and feet and sharp stabbing pains in the palms of my hands and the soles of my feet that felt like cramp. I now know that these are a common symptom related to hyperventilation and high anxiety as carbon dioxide 'pools' in the extremities, but back then they scared me, were hellishly painful and totally unexplained. The doctors and psychologists thought I was making it up and those who believed me thought that the pain was psychosomatic. But they were real and common symptoms with an explainable source. My symptoms were based on a simple physiology but that eluded the so-called professionals.

Even on good days I felt as if I had the flu. I felt sweaty, weak and shaky with heavy legs and limb pain.

I became obsessed with my heart again and constantly took my pulse. I don't know what I was supposed to be feeling for, as the pulse can't tell you anything about your condition when used as an isolated method of diagnosis. This is a common practice amongst anxiety sufferers, again a form of reassurance or safety-seeking behaviour.

My anxious mind wanted to check that I was still alive; it made no sense at all. I continued to feel my pulse regularly and only stopped when my condition started to improve, which was much later on. Also much later, I observed a young man on a train doing the exact same thing while looking very anxious indeed. He looked perfectly healthy and I felt I knew exactly what he was going through. I wanted to talk to him about it but couldn't find the words to start the conversation. I now know that there are hundreds of millions of people just like him and me.

Sometimes my lips would tingle and I would feel like a powerful electric current was being passed through me. These sensations would usually affect my arms, my legs, my chest, neck or back. As they became stronger and faster they would take my breath away, and on one occasion, they were so powerful that I was thrown across the room. Its power was immense and overwhelming and when it hit, it felt like lightening. It's incredible what levels of physical manifestations of anxiety are achievable as adrenaline is fired out during the anxiety control mechanism.

Beth would come home at night and lift me from the sofa or the floor. I was hardly able to stand, if we could get outside, she would walk me around the garden as I hung onto her, hardly able to breathe, scared for my life.

Even walking down the passageway from the living room to the bathroom would mean having to support myself against the wall as I walked, otherwise I would veer from side to side as if I were drunk.

Preparing food or drinks was too scary to attempt, if I fell or had a panic attack, I would be too far from the telephone to call for help. Of course, the reality was that these anxious scenarios of impending death were figments of my anxious imagination, but how I was supposed to know or understand that when it all felt so real and so overwhelming. My mind was telling me I was under threat of imminent death and the symptoms strongly backed up that notion. It all seemed so real, so current and so raw.

The funny thing is that had I called anyone, they probably wouldn't have come to me, Beth couldn't keep leaving work and the rest of my family had never come when I had called them previously. I felt so, so isolated.

I tried to leave the house on numerous occasions but unless I was with someone I felt that I just couldn't do it. I got to the corner shop once but had to call Beth who eventually came out to fetch me. I just froze. I was so scared. The owners and customers in the shop thought that I was completely crazy as I held on to the counter for dear life, panting and holding my chest. The feelings were still so intense, the chest pains and muscle spasms were so real.

OK, in the previous twelve months I had experienced periods of feeling less anxious and more positive but these had coincided with social circumstances: meeting Beth, work circumstances and prescription drugs. I knew the drugs weren't helping my recovery but they would at least 'dope me up' at the onset, which offered temporary relief sometimes.

Searching for a cure

I started to use the Internet more as and when I felt capable. The Internet was not only a distraction but also a source of information about anxiety and panic attacks. Just to know that people around the world suffered in the same way gave me comfort and reassurance that I was not alone. If only I could have talked to these other people. It wasn't until later that I realised that, while knowledge is a powerful thing, it can also be destructive. An anxious person can become consumed in the cycle of constant research and not everything on the Internet is what anxious people want to hear. Misinformation can cause an anxiety sufferer to become more anxious.

Anxiety forums and discussion groups are an anxiety sufferer's worst enemy because only anxious people use them, and most of them are long-term sufferers who are bitter and desperate. The last thing a sufferer needs is to become like them, to become entrenched in a dialogue with other sufferers and to become enveloped by negativity.

There are many resources that masquerade as 'caring organisations' and even charities but when the chips are down, turn into vicious, vindictive and damaging enemies. Over the years I have fallen prey to many who have a vested interest in keeping people anxious.

Aged twenty-six, eighteen stone, terrified and medicated.

What you experience, the things you expose yourself to in life, you become. It doesn't matter what reassurance these resources offer, exposing yourself to them is counterproductive. They are supportive of your anxiety and not your recovery.

Coitus unpleasantus

Sex ... how attractive can it possibly be to watch an overweight man, sit on the end of the bed checking his pulse in his neck after sex or stop, or even slow down, halfway through for a pulse-taking interlude? It's laughable now but at the time, despite wanting to have a normal sex life or any life in truth, I was attempting to give Beth as much normality as possible and whilst the will was strong, the mind and body were weak.

I kept envisaging the scene of firemen dragging my lifeless body off Beth after they had entered the building forcefully and found her pinned beneath my lardy backside. Seriously, this scene played out in my mind during the act! It's laughable now but at the time it seemed plausible.

Most sufferers have issues around sex: 'What if I have a heart attack?' 'What if I can't breathe?' 'What if I can't enjoy it?' 'What if I can't make my partner enjoy it?' 'What if I am gay?' These questions and others have been heard thousands of times by my team and myself, and underline the fact that when you are in a high-anxiety state, the mind isn't focused on sex, enjoyment or lust; instead, the mind is focused on potential risk.

In fact, this concept is true of everything anxious people do from reading to exercising from socializing to sex; the subconscious mind is always focused on threat, never on the task at hand.

The anxiety response developed to protect us against true risk and during the anxiety response (flight or fight) the physical and psychological systems involved in pleasure responses is suspended, so even if you wanted to enjoy sex, intimacy or pleasure, the mind and body conspire to make it, more or less, impossible.

Even those sex acts that didn't involve 'exercise' were enough to send 'what if' thoughts reeling through my head. I would worry that it would effect my endocrine system or that I would contract a disease. I must have considered hundreds of scenarios, not just about sex but about every conceivable catastrophic outcome possible and they would replay like a film on a loop over and over again – so graphic, seeming so real, seeming so normal and yet some of them were 'way out there' when compared with the logical truth.

As the months past and I gradually reduced my doses of Diazepam. I noticed very slight improvements in my symptoms and started going out more. I didn't travel far but, accompanied, I could go to the local shops, out for a meal occasionally and to family events.

Sometimes, I coped quite well with only the normal chest, breathing and muscle spasms while at other times I panicked and felt quite ill, but I got through it. However, it also wasn't unusual for me to end up in the pub toilet splashing my face with water as my family sat next-door ignoring my plight. Beth held my hand tightly under the table, how could I have survived without her?

I started to notice that eating larger amounts of certain foods affected the severity of my anxiety. Later, I realised that his was due to changes in blood sugar levels, controlled by insulin release, and also restricted breathing and hyperventilation, which we now know is common in anxiety sufferers. The endocrine system that controls hormones is implicated in every bodily system as it sends out these chemical messengers to activate and assist in every system from digestion to thought.

During the high-anxiety response these systems are modified, manipulated, activated or deactivated in order for the body and mind to focus on real threat. Many sufferers lose their appetite, lose their libido, are unable to concentrate on simple tasks like reading or writing and when they come to us asking why, the answer is simple. Think about it, why would you want to have sex or read a book while fighting a tiger?

The anxiety response (the emotion of fear) developed to shut off unnecessary systems while it identifies and deals with REAL threat. The response and focus is strong and fixed until the threat subsides. When real threat is present and the anxiety response is appropriate, this focus lasts, maybe, a few minutes and is then deactivated once the threat has gone. In an anxiety disorder, where no REAL threat is present and the anxiety is perpetuated by other means (which I will talk about shortly), these systems run constantly without deactivation; and it is this that causes the constant and tiring cycle of symptoms and thoughts.

During an anxiety disorder, the sufferer loses sight of the truth amidst the bombardment of symptoms and thoughts, which in the context of 'normality' and physical and psychological status quo, have no logical conclusion. The problem is that when the body and mind are affected by the flight-or-fight response and bodily systems are being manipulated to fight threat, all of those systems are, for a short time at least, out of 'sync'. This is fine when anxiety is appropriate and the response is short lived, but when it is perpetuated during an anxiety 'disorder', those short term 'glitches' in systemic balance can become troublesome – not damaging – TROUBLESOME. Every symptom – from aching muscles, neck pain and numbness to a racing heart, digestive upsets and inappropriate thoughts – is the result of that prolonged anxiety response, not the symptoms of other illnesses.

It is so difficult for sufferers to believe they are safe despite all of the symptoms because while the anxiety response causes all these symptoms, it also causes the activation of the fear response risk assessment 'what if' questions, which also confirms, wrongly, that those symptoms are threatening. This is the train crash that results from the design flaw in human evolution that allows our advanced creative intellect to influence the emotion of fear – a double-edged sword.

Not-so-restful sleep and digestion issues

I continued to experience panic during the night and only slept for perhaps two to four hours per night on average. I would experience bouts of terrifying 'night frights', most people have experienced these at some time, suddenly waking, heart racing like a steam train, beads of sweat trickling from everywhere, shaking, shortness of breath, terror – a scary and frustrating experience but totally harmless.

The subconscious mind never sleeps. In addition to regulating all of your autonomic systems like breathing, circulation, digestion and the endocrine system while your conscious mind sleeps, it also manages your emotions and thoughts. Just because your conscious mind is sleeping it doesn't mean that your thoughts aren't generating anxious scenarios, responding to sensations, which are perceived as threats, and creating inappropriate anxiety responses.

Often, as I woke with a panic attack, I would have incredibly complex thoughts, scenarios or images in my mind's eye. These would sometimes be terrifying. I would get out of bed, grab a spare duvet, lie on the sofa comfortably watching some, fairly innocuous TV programme, so as not to stimulate my brain further, and there I would fall back to sleep, diverted by the TV 'data' slightly and comfortable enough to sleep through the night.

Other times I would lie there for hours before falling asleep again but it was a far more productive way to achieve rest; lying in a dark room next to another sleeping person with only anxious thoughts to keep you company is not a productive environment for an anxious person, insomnia sufferer or anyone else for that matter.

After four months I was taking a reduced dose of Diazepam three times a day which, I decided, would be reduced by firstly eliminating my midday dose followed in three weeks time by the morning dose and then the night time dose, and that is exactly what I did.

My digestion was still poor, I found out later that it would never be perfect again; Diazepam had artificially relaxed my stomach and intestines for so long that when I stopped taking it, my digestion couldn't cope. The drugs and my anxiety had irreversibly affected my stomach's nerves, which assist the movement and digestion of food in the intestines.

My digestive system could no longer cope with the types of food that I was able to eat before my illness. Spicy food, bulky, stodgy food and hot foods badly affected me and I started to realise that eating made me feel worse. This worried me immensely; I thought I would develop an eating disorder if I didn't eat correctly.

I now know that Benzodiazepine withdrawal causes a drop in blood sugar level. Eating boosts your blood sugar level but because my system was so confused, I would experience extreme sugar highs quickly followed by extreme lows, my energy levels seesawed and I felt quite unwell.

I started getting what is commonly referred to as 'dumping syndrome' or 'rapid gastric emptying'. I would feel full very early on in a meal with restriction in my chest and shortness of breath. Then I would have to rush to the toilet within minutes.

Over the next few weeks, I experimented using a process of elimination to discover which foods I could tolerate. Finally, I discovered that starchy foods were the main source of the problem. I eliminated potatoes, bread and pasta from my diet and my symptoms improved quite quickly. I still have to be careful about what I eat, but the condition is much more manageable.

I knew that I now had to start reducing my dose of Stelazine. I did this over the next two months and fortunately experienced very little rebound anxiety. As you can imagine, this was such a relief as I had feared a repeat performance of the Diazepam withdrawal, but it never came.

I only discovered, recently, that this condition has a name, Benzodiazepine

Withdrawal Syndrome. I knew I had the syndrome and what had caused it, but had never realised it was a separate and recognised medical condition.

Although I was nearly drug free, my anxiety was still horrendous but at least I was beginning to understand what was anxiety related and what was drug related. Separating the two sets of symptoms was interesting and enlightening.

Cognitive Behavioural Therapy (CBT)

I decided to enrol the help of an anxiety-management counsellor and contacted a cognitive behavioural therapist, who had been highly recommended by the British Association of Chartered Psychotherapists. The association was very helpful and supplied me with a list of the best therapists in the country. It was pure coincidence that one of them was based about 15 miles from where I lived. Cognitive therapy, or CBT, uses a series of homework-based exercises to reintroduce anxiety-provoking situations and teach coping strategies to use when feeling anxious. It is also meant to teach you to alter your thought processes and challenge irrational beliefs about your anxiety.

The sessions gave me the opportunity to talk to an impartial third person about anything that had contributed to my condition. Did this help me? No ... it was the chance for a nice chat but did it cure me or lessen my anxiety? Not at all, in fact I was getting worse.

The problem with cognitive therapy (CBT), which is not like conventional therapy where you sit and talk at someone for an hour, you can do that if you wish, is that you always leave the session with a bag of tools to use when at home. You'd think that sounds great wouldn't you?

But it really was a waste of time and money ... a lot of money.

This particular CBT practitioner made me read aloud sections from a CBT manual, while he sat there with an inane grin on his face. He would then set me homework in the form of 'anxiety diaries', 'anxiety rating cards' and other such techniques, which only served only to remind me consciously that I was anxious. As the weeks went on I got worse and more desperate.

I now know why and understand the science of why CBT is so very counterproductive in the treatment of high anxiety. Through long consultations, attending mental health events and discussions with hundreds of mental health professionals it is clear to see why talking therapies can be damaging. The forefathers of this science, eminent psychologists such as Karl Lange and

William James, would be confused and concerned if they could only see CBT in use with anxiety disorders.

CBT and other talking therapies demand that you ACT like an anxious person in a number of ways, for example, many CBT therapists recommend their clients to take the following actions:

- Be vigilant about your symptoms by rating them and setting time aside to consider them.

- Keep a diary of your anxiety levels throughout the day

- Note down 'negative thoughts' and attempt to then dream up alternatives.

- Avoid the things that make you anxious.

- Set aside time each day to find a quiet place in which to 'worry'.

Here is the advice from a CBT provision made available by a government health organisation available online and leaflets, which are circulated via medical centres and doctors as part of a huge NHS initiative.

Here are their CBT based 'tips' for reducing anxiety:

1. Understand more about anxiety.

2. Learn to challenge your negative thoughts and to see things more realistically.

3. Improve your ability to solve problems.

4. Learn how to reduce how much time you spend worrying.

5. Learn how you can feel more relaxed (both physically and mentally).

6. Learn how to stop avoiding the things that make you anxious.

Let me quickly explain the flaws in this plan.

1. It asks you to PRACTISE BEING ANXIOUS and constantly focus on your anxiety while perpetuating the anxious behaviours that FUEL your anxiety. Anxiety recovery is a process of forgetting not remembering.

2. It asks you to focus on the subconsciously created anxious thoughts over which you have NO control and somehow, perhaps through magic or prayer, challenge them. It asks you to 'see them in a more realistic light'. In anxiety disorders THEY ARE REAL, despite being inappropriate. By doing this you perpetuate the anxious cycle by practising being anxious.

3. It asks you to focus on your 'problems' in the midst of a high-anxiety condition. Need I explain how and why this is damaging?

4. It asks you to learn how to reduce the time you spend worrying! Are they asking you to keep a diary of the time you spend worrying or to, somehow, rewire the deepest portions of your subconscious mind in order to modify 'worry neural pathways' – what a nonsense. Later, I'll describe how you can put time aside each day as 'worry time' and collect worries throughout the day, which you can focus on during your worry time, and this is a much more helpful approach.

5. It asks you to relax – sit down, empty your mind and allow anxious thought to 'rush in', envelope you and overwhelm you mentally and physically, which is probably not great advice. Sounds really relaxing but not for a sufferer.

6. While suffering with a high-anxiety condition – OCD, agoraphobia and all of the vast array of anxious, obsessive, safety-seeking behaviours – it asks you to DO those things that most scare you because by exposing yourself to those things, you'll magically become non-anxious. Exposure therapy DOES NOT work for anxiety conditions, as all it does is reinforce the subconscious anxious memory.

When I first found this resource online, I wrote to the developers to inform them of just how dangerous, badly written, childish and inappropriate the resource was for anxiety sufferers, but they didn't respond.

What concerns me most about this advice? The fact that thousands of people rely on medical and psychological practitioners under the misapprehension that they know what they are talking about and their education and experience is enough. Educated people provide these resources and yet every single element is inappropriate, incorrect and damaging ... surely they know that ... don't they? If not then why not? If so, why do they circulate such damaging material?

Finding the key to recovery

Anxious people world-over are being treated by inappropriate psychotherapy and medication and that troubles me to my core.

One thing that seems to be common between all healthcare professionals, whether in private or general practice, is that they don't like being bothered outside of session times, so even if any of these talking therapies had any curative merit, they wouldn't provide anything like the level of support, guidance and reassurance required to create recovery in sufferers.

During this period of my life, I realised that there were many people, some I had met and some I had heard about, who were RECOVERED sufferers. This started me thinking about what it was that other people had done to overcome their disorder. Being the born researcher that I am, I decided to contact as many current and former anxiety sufferers as possible in order to interview them.

I devised a series of questions to identify the key elements of their recovery, their life practices and their mental state during their disorder, during their recovery and afterwards.

My research became an obsession. I reached out further, taking in the studies of psychologists, psychiatrists, philosophers, medics and many other 'body and mind' practitioners in order to gather the most relevant information possible.

After around two months, I had gathered so much information that our spare room looked like a mad professor's office with piles of papers and books everywhere. I even created a 'mood board' on the wall onto which I would stick anything relevant. It was like the wall of an FBI incident room.

But there was a missing 'something', a component, and although I could sense its presence in me and in the materials I had collated, I couldn't put my finger on it!

Recovery reality!

I had been stagnating at home, riddled with anxious sensations and thoughts wondering what on earth I could do to get out of the pit I was in.

I had gained so much weight and I looked horrendous but I knew that I could either live or wait to die; and if I was going to live, I made a decision that no matter what the condition threw at me, in terms of thoughts and symptoms, I would just DO.

Mum had said to me a number of times that the local volunteer centre needed some help. They had recently moved offices and needed someone to organise the centre, organise the filing and help out generally. So I phoned Maureen who looked after the centre and she told me to come along the following day.

The next day mum collected me at 10 a.m. and drove me to the centre. I sat in the car for ten minutes before I felt able to enter. My anxiety was horrendous, I could feel panic rising but I refused to allow it to get the better of me. I took a few deep breaths and entered.

I knew my mood was low that day and even though the doctor had told me that my 'anxiety with depression' would fluctuate throughout my life, I certainly wasn't prepared to accept it as fact.

Doctors and psychologists often confuse the two conditions and also often tell sufferers they have 'anxiety with depression'. This is such utter nonsense from a medical perspective because anxiety disorder is too much of the emotion of fear, while clinical depression is the complete absence of emotion, hence the requirement for chemical intervention in order to maintain and build levels of 'feel-good' chemicals in the brain.

Sure, people with high anxiety can feel very, very p***ed off with their lot but is this clinical depression? No, certainly not. Clinically depressed people often don't care less whether they live or die. Anxious people are too scared to live and too scared to die. Anxiety and depression are about as related as a headache and athlete's foot and in fifteen years of helping other anxiety sufferers, including myself, I have never met a person with an anxiety disorder and simultaneous clinical depression – it's like being happy and sad simultaneously, it just ain't possible!

Maureen had explained on the previous day that she wouldn't be there but her colleague Jane would be able to show me the ropes and explain what needed to be done.

Mum waited outside for me as I entered the centre, heart pounding, lump in throat, on the verge of a very big panic attack. I was excited to be doing something productive finally, but my anxiety had been dreadful throughout the conversation with Maureen and I really didn't know whether I could tolerate it. It seemed so much easier to stay at home and do nothing but I knew that if I did that, I wouldn't move forward with any aspect of my life.

I was determined to get to the centre and at least give it my very best shot.

The centre wasn't open by the time I arrived and as I left mum's car, I could feel the anxiety escalating as adrenaline filled my veins and the familiar tension grasped my chest. My breathing quickened as she disappeared out of sight.

She waited outside for me and, as I entered the centre, I heard a sound from behind me and turned to see Jane. We hadn't met before but I recognised her immediately. Jane was born with cerebral palsy and moved around in an electric wheelchair that she controlled with an armrest joystick. She had been briefed by Maureen about my arrival and invited me in while a friend unlocked the door.

Jane was as sharp as a needle and didn't miss a trick. She knew the office inside out and was a serious 'task master', and although she was unable to do physical work in the centre, she was, sure as hell, capable of handing out orders and delegating. She terrified me and for the first thirty minutes or so, I thought I'd just get through the ordeal and never return. I wanted to last out the day if I could because, quite honestly, I was too scared to leave.

My heart was pounding as if it would jump out of my chest and sweat poured from me but Jane didn't care as she barked out her orders. Occasionally I'd catch her smiling and I began to think she was getting a kick out of behaving so horrendously.

Jane's speech was quite severely affected by her condition, which forced me to have to listen very carefully to everything she said and as she spoke I had to concentrate on her expressions in order to get the gist of some of what she was saying. Sometimes I didn't and then I would become quite anxious, more out of embarrassment than actual fear.

Jane kept me working and by lunchtime I had finished placing the filing into alphabetical order on the shelves above Maureen's desk and had created a quick-reference index in a card file box on her desk.

Jane told me to pop out to get some lunch as her carer arrived with hers. I hadn't ventured anywhere alone for over twelve months and the thought of doing so sent my anxiety sky high again. It had been at a relatively low level all morning and it was only when I was faced with the prospect of walking up the street alone that it was reactivated.

I managed to get to the sandwich shop and returned twenty minutes later, just as Jane had finished her lunch. As soon as she saw me she barked out her orders again, which I immediately carried out without question, despite having not understood everything she had said. I soon found out that my loss of focus on her words had meant that I was taking the wrong items to the wrong place and she launched into me.

'Stupid!' she shouted.

There was no missing that. I turned to face her as she launched a barrage of new orders. This time, terrified by her again, I focused intently on her demands and carried them out without question. That's how it continued till 5 p.m. when, thank God, my mother tapped on the window. I said my goodbyes and left.

I was exhausted and decided that I would call Maureen the next day, make my excuses and move on to the next idea.

But that evening I changed my mind. The next day, I went back to the volunteer centre because what had become incredibly apparent was that when I was with Jane in that centre, my anxiety was at a lower ebb.

By lunchtime, I realised that my anxiety had reduced and the symptoms, which usually haunted me, were at a much lower level. If, according to the doctors and psychologists, I was so physically and mentally ill, how was it that by doing what I was doing, I could affect my anxiety levels? It was all falling into place in my mind.

Understanding dawns

I arrived home forty-five minutes before Beth, put a chicken in the oven, and prepared vegetables. At 6.30 p.m. Beth returned home and we ate about half-an-hour later. Beth said nothing about my having prepared dinner; something I hadn't done for years but inside she knew something was different.

Later, I lay in bed thinking until after 1 a.m. when I finally fell asleep.

I didn't notice that my anxiety was at a much lower level than it had been on previous evenings, sufferers never seem to recognise high points, but at 2 a.m. I was woken from a deep sleep by a massive panic attack that made me jump from the bed shouting as the sleep cleared and consciousness came very quickly.

Once the extreme symptoms disappeared, I lay down on the sofa and a notion started to develop in my mind. I had often wondered why it was that a condition, which is described by psychologists and medics as mental illness – requiring, so they said, a chemical solution as well as psychological devices like therapy, which is deemed by them to be incurable and chronic – should become less apparent and also less troublesome when the sufferer's mind is occupied by tasks or by emotionally 'expensive' responses. I had started to notice something that even in the midst of high anxiety or even panic, when something potentially more dangerous happened, the anxiety would subside. Of course it would always return after the event had ended.

There were a number of elements that came to me that night. They would need
to be understood more deeply and tested but they were significant to me and
ultimately vital to my recovery and to the tens of thousands of people I have
cured using them since.

I then started to realise that the emotion of fear was unsustainable under very
specific environmental circumstances.

I started to think about how I responded when people made comments or asked
about how I was feeling. I realised I intellectualised the words, I would feel OK,
but as soon as my mind was focused on how I felt, the symptoms would worsen.
It obviously took conscious focus to fuel the high-anxiety state. I am sure you
will identify with this too.

It became very apparent that the 'what if' thoughts activated during high
anxiety were searching questions, which identified and responded to risk. But
what data were they gathering? I realised that when a 'what if' manifested in
me, the thoughts that ensued would be catastrophic, reinforced by anxious
flights of fancy. I think you probably know exactly what I mean.

I turned my mind to my responses. CBT told me that by changing my thoughts I
could change my emotional responses – which I now know is utter rubbish.
That's just not how the mind works. Imagine how long we'd survive if conscious
thought had to precede the emotional response: 'Look a tiger is running at me,
what shall I do? Run? Fight? Cry?' See my point? Tiger food!

It's ludicrous that a so-called treatment should use such flawed science to justify
the fees. I was angry, but despite all the wasted time and money, CBT had been
valuable to me and it was at this point that I realised why.

CBT had taught me what doesn't work!

Although I had ignored the lesson behind this fact for years because of my total
focus on how I was feeling, I had missed the fact that it held the key to my
recovery.

You see, the subconscious part of the mind that activates the flight-or-fight
mechanism, the emotion of fear, is independent in every way in that it controls
the response without *any* conscious interaction. Imagine how it would be if we
could think our way out of an emotion? It would be so easy to say 'anxiety OFF'.
Like respiration, circulation, digestion, hormone release and every other
element of the autonomic system, the anxiety-control mechanism didn't take
orders from the conscious mind; it takes data from the senses. In other words,

your senses tell it what your body is experiencing environmentally and responds accordingly.

This was it. The solution.

Take free diving, in which the diver descends down 100 metres into the sea, or breath-holding records in which the diver doesn't draw a breath for twenty-two minutes. How is this possible? Could you do it? Is it down to a natural ability? Do these people have gills?

A free diver doesn't jump into the water and descend 100 metres on day one. Over time they expose themselves to deeper and deeper depths while training above the water to improve the way their internal organs interact in order to stay alive in those conditions. This is how we become fitter, lose weight or learn to drive. In fact, it's how humans learn any new skill. It's called neuroplasticity. Neuroplasticity is the process by which the brain creates, modifies and renders obsolete the 'hard wiring' in the brain that creates thought and memory.

So a free diver is constantly and slowly exposing their body to an increasingly life-threatening and hostile environment and as they do so, their senses feed data back to their subconscious, which modifies their internal systems in order to keep them alive. The heart rate drops, meaning they require less oxygen, which supports the fact that they cannot take a breath anyway. The diver's body metabolises stored oxygen in the blood to preserve it and their other main systems, like digestion, are slowed to prevent resources from being used up.

You see, the subconscious doesn't know when it will get more oxygen. Even though the diver may know consciously that it will be twelve or thirteen minutes they can't communicate that verbally to the subconscious any more than the 'thought-changing' exercises in CBT can modify the anxiety response.

This is all very real and proven science albeit a simplified explanation but more importantly it has been proven as a result of my recovery and that of every person I have helped.

If I had ever found an exception, I'd mention it now, trust me. This is why doctors, psychologists and organisations world over refer clients to us and why people travel from every corner of the world to attend one of our workshops or retreats.

So, if your internal systems and, more importantly, your emotions rely on sensory data fed to them by your eyes, ears, nose, mouth and skin in order to activate and then be appropriately administered, do you see how easy it can be to stop an anxiety disorder?

It's so, so easy *if* you know how. There is a true and total cure for anxiety disorders but more importantly and vital to you right now, it will remove the 'disorder' and create total 'order' – you will be better than you have ever been before. This isn't my science, it's just science. Currently, you are a Ferrari delivering milk door to door – engine revving away excitedly, ready to spin away at 200 mph – but instead, you move ten metres, stop, deliver milk and move to the next house.

When recovery has happened in you (and it will), you will become so incredibly focused, resilient and capable.

How do I know this? Because I have never seen it NOT happen.

But why did my body continue to reactivate the anxiety response? This was a key question that, once answered, completed the structure of the recovery process.

CHAPTER FOURTEEN

The Key to Total Anxiety Recovery – Putting It All Together

I NOW UNDERSTOOD what activates high-anxiety conditions. It was simply the processes that come into play within the anxiety-control mechanism and how the sensory organs are the 'data gatherers' from which the anxiety control centre receives information with which to understand the external environment and make appropriate decisions about how to respond.

I now just needed to understand why, in anxiety disorders, a cycle is created that then prevents the anxiety-recovery mechanism from switching off.

The anxiety response sends out 'what if' notions to assess real risk, I understood deeply how those 'feel' because I had experienced every single one of them. Despite every single sufferer and medical professional saying to me that they were 'thoughts', I knew, instinctively, that they were not. You have them too and yours will be specific to you and your own circumstances.

Thoughts are chunks of data pulled from memory or created as data that are received from the senses, analysed and sorted by the subconscious mind.

'What if' risk assessments are created by the autonomic nervous system and are 'notions' rather than organised thoughts. These notions take the form of chemical and electrical nerve impulses sent out to the sensory organs asking them to retrieve environmental data to be used in order to assess risk. In other words, your senses look at the situation and decide how to respond. These thoughts have no language: the subconscious has no concept of language or of the external environment and relies solely on this sensory feedback mechanism.

During flight-or-fight response, as the body prepares to take evasive or direct action against a potential threat, these 'notions' are sent out constantly asking

'What if?' 'What now?' Then, as the sensory data required to make such decisions is received, it is analysed and a packet of 'action data' is sent out, immediately in order to prepare the body and activate the appropriate areas of the body in order to carry out the response.

This process is what causes the anxiety disorder.

This all sounds great doesn't it and in principle, and up to a certain tipping point in human evolution, this worked 'a treat', but what the human blueprint didn't have a contingency plan for, was our massive tip towards social evolution.

Since the dawn of mankind, humans have evolved to interact more effectively with their environments. As the world passes through its own evolutionary timeline, we have evolved in many ways in order to remain safe on our planet. In the last few thousand years, however, this process of physical evolution has been overtaken by our social evolution – which, in the last few hundred years, has been expedited exponentially as a response to enormous scientific advancements.

Think about your own social position. What would a person of your gender and age have been capable of in 200 BC, in 600 AD, in 1500, in 1850, in 1950? What are your abilities now? Are they comparable?

In 1850, for example, a man of my age, if indeed he had reached my age, would perhaps, if he was particularly capable and very lucky to have been born into an affluent family, have become an engineer or a scientist but *most* of the men in 1850's Britain would have been workhorses in factories or mines, capable intellectually of little more than the jobs they did day in and day out.

Now, even if a man chooses a mundane or simple job role, he is generally far more spatially aware, resourceful, technically capable, socially aware and creative.

A larger proportion of society in the developed world has, through human evolution and social conditioning, become what I call 'creative intellectuals'. Most people can now, given time, turn their hand to most tasks. Many people have become property developers having never worked or trained in building skills. They have used their creative intellect to develop those skills through data gathering, trial and error and a steep and yet profitable learning curve.

This is not to say that everyone has the ability to become great, as society still has its plodders, and they are vital to our social structure but even they are far more intellectually and socially advanced than equivalent members of society in the nineteenth century.

These facts lead me to a very important realisation; it led me to understand why anxiety disorders have become a pandemic. Why they, to my mind, are the most damaging health-related problems in the world, fading clinical illness into oblivion by comparison.

They cost the UK government alone, billions of pounds each year and are responsible for more absenteeism, loss of productivity, breakdowns of family relationships and emotional damage than any other condition in the world.

And it's all preventable and curable and quickly too.

The realisation that led me to develop the only humanly possible cure for high-anxiety conditions is this: the unplanned and unavoidable nuclear explosion that happens within our physiology and psychology when our advanced creative intellect interacts with the anxiety-response mechanism is the 'fusion reaction' that perpetuates high-anxiety conditions such as generalised anxiety disorder, panic disorder, agoraphobia, obsessive compulsive disorder, pure O, derealisation, depersonalisation, eating disorders, phobia and even myalgic encephalomyelitis (ME).

Let me explain.

A person is born with these superior traits due to the genetic blend provided by their parents, the extended, preceding genetic line and the social evolutionary factors I previously explained. This person is capable, resourceful and very creatively enabled from day one and, of course, this is subject to further enhancements and embellishments throughout life's learning curve.

Now you might be sat there right now thinking, *but I'm not clever, I didn't do well at school, I haven't had a career.*

That might all be the case but those are completely irrelevant issues. I have had people from CEO's of global organisations, actors, musicians and stay-at-home mums, men sleeping rough with PTSD and people who have cleaned houses or dug trenches as clients. All, without exception, had this genetic trait and all, without exception, recovered and realised their full potential.

You are one of those people.

These people had a predisposition to develop a high-anxiety condition. This doesn't mean that a person will definitely develop an anxiety disorder, but it does mean that if their life circumstances conspire to create the environment that activates a high-anxiety response, it is only a matter of chance as to whether they then create the anxious cycle I am about to describe.

It only takes one catalyst to activate an anxiety disorder but it takes environmental factors to force it down the correct pathway.

In my case, for example, for whatever reason, possibly separation anxiety, the emotion of fear was activated at a very early age. As soon as the anxiety response sent out a 'what if' notion, in order to assess the environment around me, my immature, naive and open mind detected risk – perhaps a risk of abandonment, injury or whatever, as I don't clearly remember that far back.

As soon as I perceived risk, more adrenaline was released and the cycle continued. Even though, at times, I must have felt safer than at others because I experienced anxiety-induced nightmares, racing heart and the situation within my family, school, etc., my 'what if' thoughts were perpetuated by my situation and the anxiety-response mechanism became reset at a much higher than appropriate 'benchmark' level. My 'what if' risk assessments resulted in my creative intellect producing 'worse case scenarios', embellishing the actual risk and even imagining risks that weren't present.

This can happen at any age and can be activated by life circumstances, but in creative intellects, it can start a spiral of self-perpetuating fear and the symptoms that constant fear produces.

As an organisation, we see many thousands of new patients each year, each one with a version of the experiences I have described in this book, many falling prey to inappropriate, time wasting, expensive therapies and many addicted to prescription medications, using alcohol or recreational drugs to self-medicate, all having no idea what is wrong with them or how to change.

In many cases, medicine and psychology have let them down.

As I compiled my research, I asked hundreds of sufferers and ex-sufferers about every aspect of their recovery and, without exception, they all aligned perfectly with my theories and so proving, back then, what The Linden Method organisation, to date, has since proven many tens of thousands of times.

This is why medical professionals call my program 'a new branch of psychological practice' – one that works. It's also why our organisation consists of some of the most highly qualified and experienced anxiety-recovery specialists, psychotherapists, psychologists and doctors of psychology.

I immediately started to build my research findings into a structured daily routine – what I believed to be, the conclusive treatment for anxiety.

My days changed as did my career

If all the recovered anxiety sufferers that I'd spoke to, and therefore *every* recovered sufferer, had done the exact same things to recover, and it had worked for them, then surely, if I did the same, it would do the same for me ... and it did and at a speed that shocked me.

By this point I was starting to feel much more confident about my condition, so I became more focused on the world and wanted to make a fresh start.

I implemented my 'Method' with total compliance.

My subconscious mind immediately started to concede, to loosen its hold on my emotions and body. I had discovered the key to turning back the clock, to undoing all of the bad practices that had lead me to 'illness', a way of resetting my subconscious.

My panic attacks stopped on day one of starting my 'routine' and the depersonalisation and derealisation followed suit.

My obsessive thoughts, which manifested with some compulsions but mostly the inappropriate sexual and aggressive thoughts at that time, reduced quickly and were completely gone in under a week.

Within days I had implemented a program that switched off the anxiety response.

It was only a matter of two weeks before I was able to lead a normal life. I worked longer hours, still feeling tired but rarely anxious.

My agoraphobia receded quickly as I started a five-day 'sub-program' to reintroduce activities I had stopped. I started with small manageable doses and so didn't induce an anxiety response and fitted in with my life and daily schedule. (I now call this program 'Journey out of Agoraphobia' and give it away for free to all Linden Method clients; and they find it so easy to use and so curatively valuable.)

I started travelling more, going away on holidays and long weekends. I lost almost all of my excess weight and didn't sense any pronounced withdrawal symptoms, as the Diazepam was re-released into my system during the withdrawal process.

I quickly returned to normality, it amazed me and my family just how fragile the line is between, what is perceived as, total 'ill health' and being completely anxiety free and well ... that works in both directions!

What cured me? What cures every single sufferer? What will cure YOU?

By accepting the reassurance and case I am presenting to you in this book or from my specialists if you join The Linden Method, you will free yourself from the fear of fear that grips you each day.

By talking to my staff or reading the 'anxiety symptoms' list in the next chapter, you will see that all of what you experience is just sensation, and not truth.

Your wonderfully advanced intellect provides the fuel for the burning embers of the emotion of fear. In this lies, not only, the cause of your anxiety disorder but also your inevitable and ultimate recovery. You can and will be anxiety-disorder free, just like me and thousands of clients, of that I couldn't be more certain.

Re-forging the old neural pathways, the anxious ones and replacing them with new, productive and non-anxious ones is simple, quick and life changing. We will show you how to do this fast and you will be shocked at just how much simpler that process is than what you might currently imagine.

Your mind developed during human evolution to be an information vacuum. In anxiety disorders, your mind becomes so distracted by false fear and the myriad of physical symptoms that your logic, freedom of movement and will is severely impeded. In the Linden Method we show you how to remove that blockage and become the person you were born to be.

Through a constant, seamless cycle of compliance and the factors above, the subconscious does what it's supposed to do, as it does with 'free diving'. The mind takes on the new data and adjusts itself and your physical self quickly to mirror the external environment. It switches off the fear. It's so simple but also completely non-threatening. In fact, you will most probably enjoy it immensely. Most people do!

Don't get off the ski lift till your skis go past horizontal

Recovery is a process and, just like any other, if you stop before it's completed then you run a very high chance of falling back again. Just like a ski draglift: golden rule number one is don't let go of the lift until you have reached the summit and your skis have gone past the tipping point. The brain has the capacity to cure your anxiety but once that cure has been executed fully, the curative process will have installed a 'firewall' or 'anti-virus' software in your brain that will detect and deal with future anxiety-provoking stimuli for the rest of your life.

Because you will have been through the full recovery process and because you will have imprinted that process on your subconscious through experience, your brain will now respond differently to incoming anxious data.

Boredom is anxiety's most powerful ally. Despite being busy, people can be 'busy bored'. Activity is not intellectual challenge.

Since I recovered, I have experienced loss, danger and other potential anxiety-inducing experiences but have never become anxious again. In fact, people couldn't believe that I was the one who dealt with these experiences better than everyone else. My brain has this 'firewall' that prevents me from ever developing a high-anxiety condition.

I have been stranded up mountains on skis at 6,000 feet at dusk in a white out. I have had a car crash that could have ended disastrously. I have had many very close members of my friends and family die. But every time, I have dealt with it and moved on, anxiety free.

Anxiety disorders are cruel but curable. I will repeat this time and time again until you understand this fact. Despite how long you have suffered, how you feel, how old you are, what you see as the 'cause' of your suffering, you can be anxiety free – you will be anxiety free.

You can be normal, strong and independent one minute and plunged into anxiety the next but I would never have thought that the journey back to being completely well again could be so fast. My former psychologist even commented when he saw me in town one day. He said that he was shocked to see me outside and looking so well again when I had been, as he put it, 'so chronically ill'.

When I asked why he was shocked, he said that he thought I would never be well again and that he had almost given up on me as a lost cause. He also asked what I had done to achieve this incredible turn-around and I replied, 'Do you honestly think I would tell you?'

Why should I, his incompetence cost me a house re-mortgage, twelve wasted months and a bankruptcy. I was saving my information for the folks that matter … YOU.

Looking back

I was completely drug free within six weeks and now I look back at my time on Diazepam, Prozac, Zispin, Stelazine and all those other drugs with anger and disgust. If there were any justice in the world I would be eligible for some sort of compensation.

Looking back I know now that my 'illness' was totally misdiagnosed, mismanaged and brushed aside by a series of medical practitioners. It took five years to find a doctor who understood the condition enough to advise me wisely and knew what to do to support me, but it took my own tenacity and research to find the solution.

We often place too much trust in the hands of so-called professional people, believing their judgement unquestionably. We hardly ever ask for a second opinion, discuss what our prescription is, what it does and its possible risks. We think that just because a person has a degree, has patients, makes diagnoses and prescribes medication, that they know what they are doing and actually care about it. I am living proof that sometimes this presumption can be very, very wrong.

If only I had discovered this Method earlier, if only I had discovered it when I was thirteen or sooner. I lost nearly a decade of my life to severe anxiety and seventeen years of my early life to fluctuating anxiety disorders that could have al been avoided.

At the Linden Centres we help children as young as eight years old and when I see how their lives are transformed and when I see them go from terrified to happy, I think of myself at the same age and remember the fears that dominated every waking moment of my life till I was twenty-seven years old.

I was not force fed the tablets I was prescribed; I took them of my own free will because I wanted to recover and I trusted those who advised me under the misguided assumption that they were correct.

In over four years of taking Diazepam, I never once received a printed instruction leaflet with my prescription, I was not informed of the side effects or recommended period of use; that was the doctors responsibility and it was ignored. I hold the doctors I visited totally responsible for the resultant illness, they still work, live eat and sleep well at night, collect large pay cheques, go on holiday and have relatively normal lives.

I now teach other people how to achieve what I achieved. I have 'A list' actors, musicians, politicians and other high-profile clients in my list of cured clients, many of whom have become personal friends, and all of whom refer people to me in a constant stream.

An anxiety pandemic

Most sufferers have not become addicted to medications but take them under the guidance of their doctors. You wouldn't believe how many people come out of the woodwork and admit to having panic attacks or anxiety when the subject arises. We are living in an anxiety pandemic and people I have known for a considerable amount of time, through work for example, have come to me for a confidential chat about the strange sensations they are experiencing and have hidden their condition for years, even from me. It seems to be becoming more and more prevalent.

My work with media, TV, newspapers, magazines and radio worldwide has meant that we now reach more and more sufferers in order to reassure them that they can and will be cured and in order to spread the word that this pandemic can be eliminated.

I have shown time and time again that what we do is THE solution – a number of hugely profitable industries exist to sell products for the treatment of cut skin but there is only one cure for cut skin and that is the body's ability to send new skin cells to the gap. The same is true of anxiety disorders. Your body will, with our help, cure itself.

As I write this, I am sat at a table on a Mediterranean island where I have been for three weeks with my family. I am lucky to be able to work from where I am, wherever I find myself. Last week a desperate mum flew her son to see me here fearing that if she waited for my return her son would be hospitalised. Frequent requests for help mean that I often fly around the world to attend clients in businesses, TV and film studios, recording studios and other high-profile locations ... but I am just me and can only do so much.

I believe the programs and resources we provide to be the best money can buy at prices everyone can afford and I hope that one day The Linden Method will be available to every sufferer.

Our clients come from every corner of the globe. We have as many clients in Australia and Asia as across North, South and Central America and the Middle East. It's a wonderful thing to be part of.

Analysing my techniques fully and identifying every factor that helped me return to normal has enabled me to pinpoint exactly what techniques do and don't work for every sufferer.

Trial Results – True confirmation of our program's efficacy

Analysis of the success of our programs resulted in a trial being undertaken by Martin Jensen using statistical analysis software at Copenhagen University.

Taking a large group of anxiety sufferers Martin led a trial that saw the group go through The Linden Method and here are the results.

Incoming patients had an average anxiety level of 18.24 out of 21, which is classed as severe. This was tested using the GAD7 anxiety scale, the UK government recognised tool for gauging anxiety levels.

The subjects then did The Linden Method.

After they had completed The Method (average one month), their anxiety levels were measured again.

The average anxiety level was now 2.84 out of 21 where 5 is 'normal', so 2.84 is better than normal.

No other anxiety-disorder treatment comes close to these results. This makes me so proud of what we do and the lives we change.

Here are some comments from the people involved in the trial. Names have been removed due to confidentiality laws.

I honestly believe that the program will work for everyone who uses it. It changed my life. I hope this method spreads worldwide to allow everyone to be healed from anxiety problems. Even their quality of life will change for the better so go ahead and please continue helping people.

This should be available to everyone. Its benefits are massive and it is reassuring. Understanding my condition and its manifestations were made clear to me via The Linden Method. I cannot recommend highly enough the relief and support I have received. Every sufferer should receive this.

This would save the health service millions in drug costs, GP visits counselling and other related costs – for example paying benefits to people unable to work due to anxiety-related conditions. More importantly this Method gives people their lives back – anxiety is the most unpleasant and debilitating experience I have ever experienced. Believe me, I've tried many different things and none of them worked until I used this method.

The Linden Method is one of the best things that have happened to me in my life. I finally have my life back. If you are on the fence about it or doubting that it will work, just think of how many things you have tried that didn't work. I promise you it will work. Just listen and do the program and you will be on your way to recovery. It is such a wonderful feeling. I would rather do this than be on medications any day of my life. I would think you would want the same. God Bless Charles and his team.

I have no doubt in my mind that this would be a viable and effective treatment to offer on the NHS and have no qualms about recommending it. You can ask my family and friends, but it should be enough to ask me, I am completely transformed! I have an amazing GP, and was given CBT counselling through the NHS (I also paid for it privately!), and although this helped me 'manage' my anxiety and OCD it did not lessen it. The Linden Method seriously has 'cured' me. I worry a normal amount about 'normal and real things'. (In fact I would say I probably worry a little less than those around me, which is just amazing!)

I truly hope The Linden Method becomes available through doctors – I work and pay taxes, and would be very happy to think that my taxes go towards a way to cure people from this debilitating and misunderstood disorder.

The only thing that scares me these days is the fact that there are people out there going through what I went through that are not aware that this method exists/works. No one should have to live with anxiety. This could save the thousands of lives being wasted."

Once you master it, it will become like a walk in the park! Honestly, everything makes so much sense, just read, read and read away. Why would you want to become dependant on medication, which only puts a hold on your troubles, when you can cure yourself with out medication!

I would firstly like to say a very big thank you to Charles and Beth. I am slowly getting my friends back as I deserted all of them and starting to live again. I would not recommend anything for anxiety apart from The Linden Method, all these other therapies do not work, fact! Kind regards.

This method changed my life. I wish everyone could learn this method because their lives would change for the better – even non-anxious people. Please try your best to spread The Linden Method and please try to translate into Arabic because we have a lot of cases and I am willing to help in any way. Thank you.

It is the best money you'll ever spend, if it is the money that is putting you off. It saved my life and I am now studying Holistic Therapy and Stress Management. My anxiety started three and a half years ago when I was twenty-one, after having been involved in a bad car accident. Luckily I found The Linden Method having only had anxiety for a year. But it was 1 year too long! Although looking at it now, it is the best journey I've ever been through! I feel amazing now!

CBT and medication had both failed. I now feel more positive than I have felt in thirty years. I can honestly say that since completing the program I now look forward to each day without the stomach churning and awful feeling of impending doom. I would recommend The Linden Method wholeheartedly and would be happy to provide further information should it be required.

Before The Linden Method I wasn't able to eat for fear of swallowing, I lost tons of weight and my mum was worried that I'd end up hospitalised. I also suffered from daily panic attacks and high anxiety – I couldn't switch my brain off. I would skip meals out with friends as I just wanted to hide away in my room. I didn't know how to get my life back, I tried counselling but it only improved things slightly. I still believed there was something physically wrong with me and I couldn't get these negative thoughts out of my head. I was at my lowest point in life when I came across The Linden Method and I'm glad I did. It didn't take long before the panic attacks stopped and I started feeling myself again. Now I go out for meals with friends and family and am enjoying my life again. I have also been approached by others suffering from high anxiety and panic attacks and have recommended this method to them. It really does work!

Hi everyone, this is the cure for anxiety disorder. I am talking from my personal experience. I went to many doctors but they were no use at all. They have wrong treatment. This treatment is the one that cures anxiety disorders completely and it is a simple process. God bless Charles Linden.

The Linden Method gave me hope, motivation to get well, an understanding of myself and literally saved my life. I can't praise Charles, Beth and his team enough.

I never visited a GP or anything, I was always too embarrassed to reveal my feelings and thoughts, I just Internet searched and thankfully gave The Linden Method a shot and it worked or works(!) really well for me. I implement it in my behaviour daily, and have a wonderful knowledge of the behaviour related to anxiety conditions now thanks to Charles. I also use what I have learnt to help all my young children through stressful periods or change!

If I had had The Linden Method available to me fifteen years ago it would have saved fifteen years of, quite frankly, misery! I tried every treatment out there on the NHS and every other weird and wonderful therapy but nothing worked until I found The Linden Method. I even lost my colon and developed alopecia because of the stress. The method is the only program that is curative as it forces the curative process to happen, rather than handing out pointless coping strategies and medications that don't work. Couldn't rate this program any higher. Complete lifesaver. Must be able to access this on the NHS and save so many peoples needless suffering.

Having suffered from anxiety since the age of fifteen – having been to see my GP on too many numerous occasions to count, having had every blood test under the sun, having been prescribed propranolol, having been to see a CBT counsellor of my own accord – the only treatment that actually cured my anxiety was The Linden Method. I attended the residential course when I was suffering from daily if not hourly panic attacks and can hand on heart state that I have not had one panic attack since completing course. This method is simple, drug free, highly effective and in my opinion should definitely be an option for all patients.

I have to thank God and Charles for this method. Before I was not able to walk out of my house. I had that horrible sensation that I could not breathe and I would die. It took me almost four weeks to understand how every thing works!! It was hard but I did it! Thank you Charles now I am 100 per cent cured!! The mind is the most powerful thing on Earth!!!

I just followed the program and within a month or so I was no longer having the anxiety. Thank you for your program. I was really scared and when you said it was not a mental illness that did more to calm me than anything. My mother was in a mental institution all my life and I was always afraid I would be like her. When the anxiety came, I attached more danger than normal. I did The Linden Method and I no longer fear that I will be like my mother.

The staff at The Linden Method have been my guardian angels! They have helped me so much, with their on-going support, calming effects; they really helped put me on the right path and simply have been amazing! And I thank them all from the bottom of my heart! They explain what's going on with you, which helps you to understand, and with understanding there is less anxiety. I would highly recommend to anyone with anxiety issues.

This is the ONLY method that worked for me – I tried CBT, counselling, mindfulness, hypnosis, acupuncture, homeopathic medicines and nothing helped me/my symptoms of anxiety. I would recommend TLM to anybody suffering with anxiety.

I wished I had discovered this earlier because it has made such a difference to my life. The Linden Method would amaze everyone with an anxiety problem, and it would just save years of endless searching and getting the wrong advice. If my doctor had access to The Linden Method It would have been a lifesaver.

I was an absolute wreck all the way through the ten to fifteen years that I suffered with anxiety and severe panic, even on medication! Don't get me wrong, medication helped me relax and block it out the odd time but it always came back with a vengeance, I found out about The Linden Method online and ordered it, and I can honestly say that it's the best-spent money in my entire life. I didn't even follow the whole thing through but only read what I needed to, to make me understand! I am now medication free ... enjoying life the way I never thought I would be able to do eve again. The only panic/anxiety cure is, by far ... The Linden Method.

I suffered with anxiety for twenty-five years and I honestly thought that there was no way out. I had been in the Priory on several occasions and although some of the techniques I learned helped lessen the anxiety for a month or two it would always come back. This may have been as all we talked about was how our day/week had been and how anxious we all were. TLM has worked for me. This method really works and I would urge others to use it, it gave me my life back.

Living life how it's meant to be lived

I am now forty-six, married to Beth and we have two gorgeous children, Charlie and Florence, with whom I can enjoy every moment anxiety free, with whom I can travel, play and enjoy life to the full without considering the sensations and thoughts that once plagued me.

If anyone tells you that you are incurable and that anxiety management and coping strategies are the best that you can hope for, dump them. Ignorance and selfish fee building should be outlawed.

Even if the GP you have used for years, the ancient family physician, or a trusted friend who is a psychologist or doctor doesn't tell you that a cure is possible it's only because they haven't met my staff, my clients or me.

It's my dream that, one day, we will find a way to get The Linden Method to every single sufferer around the world because only that way will they see that a cure is possible and be able to assess for themselves just how easy it is to achieve.

We are well on the way to achieving this as we have launched our government recognised Anxiety Recovery Coaching qualification, which is now being taught to mental health professionals and ex clients so that we can all work together to eradicate this pandemic.

People say that The Linden Method, in addition to being the cure for high-anxiety conditions, is also 'just a great way to lead your life', and I couldn't agree more. We now have non-anxious people doing The Linden Method because they see the changes that anxious people have made – in order to become anxiety free – which have also lead them to becoming more fulfilled in every aspect of their lives.

The world offers so much and anxious people spend every day retreating from the offerings that can, in a very short space of time, provide them with a sense of excitement, challenge and fulfilment but, as I too well know, false fear prevents the challenge being met and procrastination kicks in.

Life continues

My life story continues as our family unit goes through trials of mental and physical strength and the normal experiences of life.

What has become increasingly apparent, as I observe the people who populate my ever-changing environments, is that you cannot calibrate your perceptions with others' around you: You can never know what motivates them; what their true feelings are and which of those, thoughts, feelings and actions they provoke, they wish to project onto you. Too many words are spoken with ever-increasing levels of sophisticated language, which also seem to increase in aggression. Ill prepared, and often emotionally charged, communication has become easier with advancements in communication technology and an ever-increasing group of unpoliced platforms such as social media.

As a species and as individuals, humans have shrugged off social structure and the control mechanisms that once, somewhat, preserved social etiquette and standards, and now more than ever, from a family situation in which there once existed a hierarchy of control, to a child being bullied to the point of suicide through social media, our societies are becoming lawless, threatening and loveless.

I believe that without respect, honesty and integrity, we have nothing.

I wish to preserve what was once the 'norm' and my children will grow up with the respect and values that were instilled in me. I'm not perfect, far from it, however, everyone needs to take the time to take a deep breath in a dark room, close their eyes and evaluate what they do and say – stripping away their ego, their social, economic and work situations – and just BE human for ten minutes and allow themselves to be totally honest; only this way can the truth be exposed and changes made which make life's pathway easier and far more fulfilling.

Anxiety conditions are at pandemic proportions and are so massively impactful on every aspect of life and one day the world will realise their impact, the cost, both human and economic, and realise that with forethought and honesty, rather than economic selfishness, it could have all been prevented.

I play a small but growing part in conveying that truth, helping those who are open to MY truth with our program and knowledge. My undying hope is that during a moment of honesty and clarity, a person with decision-making power will one day see that providing my cure to the tens of millions of anxiety sufferers will be more profitable than supporting the drug companies and inappropriate psychotherapeutic practices. It really is a 'no brainer' but human nature seems to support the lazy attitude to healthcare – which has been nurtured for so many years – perhaps because keeping people 'unwell' is far more profitable than allowing incredibly gifted people to access the curative resources that would make the world a far better and fulfilling place to be.

I can only offer you the chance to change the way you feel and think like I did. I can only show you the way. I KNOW how to cure anxiety disorders and have never failed to do so. It's simple. It's fast and it's permanent. The cure doesn't require great effort, or enormous life changes, just a simple change in the way you structure your days. No extra time investment. No face your fear tactics. No CBT or medication.

If it's worked for tens of thousands from age eight to ninety-four, it'll work for you too because if you are human and suffer with a high-anxiety condition, it can't fail. The only reason for failure is non-compliance and being non-compliant is a ludicrously stupid decision to make.

I sit here now, the sun is glaring through the window, my two fingers tapping away at the keyboard and when I divert my conscious mind to my inner self, I find no fear, just excitement at what today and the rest of my days might bring ... join me on that exciting journey.

CHAPTER FIFTEEN

Anxiety Symptoms ...
Or Are They?

First of all, **please let me be totally clear, the sensations and thoughts you experience during high anxiety are NOT SYMPTOMS at all, but the normal, expected physical reactions associated with the release of the emotion of fear. For ease, however, I will continue to call them *symptoms*.**

Anxiety symptoms are the result of activation of the emotion of fear, which sets off a 'chain reaction' of normal, but inappropriate, bodily functions.

Anxiety symptoms can be both physical and emotional, but it is important to note that there is not one anxiety symptom that represents any threat to a sufferer's health. After all, it wouldn't be much of a 'self-preservation' mechanism if it produced a harmful physical response. These sensations and thoughts developed to keep you safe, not to harm you in any way and are all the result of modifications that are made to you body and mind in order to prepare you to respond appropriately to REAL threat, but, of course, in a high-anxiety conditions, REAL threat doesn't exist.

Anxiety symptoms are caused by an exaggerated anxiety reaction, which is controlled by the subconscious mind in a small organ called the amygdala. This organ is responsible for controlling the internal mechanisms that cause the sufferer to experience high anxiety, panic and all of the unpleasant symptoms of anxiety they carry with them. The amygdala acts rather like a thermostat, which controls the anxiety level and is responsible for causing all of the symptoms of anxiety.

An anxiety condition has three major components that determine the kind of anxiety symptoms experienced:

First, there is a psycho-physiological (physical) component, which produces anxiety symptoms such as palpitations (racing heart), breathlessness, dizziness and sweating. This component produces anxiety symptoms that affect us on a purely psychological level and are mostly as a direct result of adrenaline release during the fight-or-fight response.

Second, there is a psychological component, characterised by anxiety symptoms such as irritability, obsessions, lack of concentration and deep feelings of fear. These anxiety symptoms may be constant or may be more intense during an anxiety attack (panic attack). Like the physiological anxiety symptoms, these are harmless but they can make the sufferer feel helpless and desperate.

Third, there may be an interpersonal component featuring an inclination to cling to other people for reassurance, support or guidance. This is because anxiety symptoms cause such a vast range of sensations and thoughts, the sufferer often withdraws socially in order to protect themselves from potentially anxiety-provoking situations and stimuli. This can cause agoraphobia, a condition that is commonly referred to as a 'standalone' condition as opposed to an anxiety symptom. Agoraphobia, like all anxiety conditions, disappears as the anxiety level is reduced during recovery. None of our clients remain agoraphobic after recovery is completed.

Common anxiety symptoms

Most people will experiences anxiety symptoms at some point during their lives, and these are usually a variation of the same group of basic symptoms, including the most common ones such as:

• Smothering sensations and shortness of breath

• Racing heart, slow heart beat, palpitations

• Chest pain

• 'Lump in throat' and difficulty swallowing

• Blanching (colour loss in the skin)

• Excessive perspiration (sweating)

• Shaking or shivering (visibly or internally)

- Pain or numbness in the head, face, neck or shoulders

- Rapid gastric emptying

- Indigestion, heartburn, constipation and diarrhoea

- Sexual dysfunction

- Loss of libido

- Symptoms of urinary tract infection

- Skin rashes

- Weakness/tingling in arms, hands or feet

- 'Electric shock' feelings (anywhere in the body)

- Dry mouth

- Insomnia

- Nightmares

- Sensory confusion (e.g. nasal cavity or mouth being perceived as enlarged)

- Fears of going mad or losing control

- Increased depression and suicidal feelings

- Aggression

- Flu-like symptoms

- Distorted vision

- Disturbed hearing

- Racing thoughts

- Hormone problems

- Headaches and feelings of having a 'tight band around head'

- Sore eyes

- Agoraphobia

- Hallucinations

- 'Creeping' or 'pins and needles' sensations in the skin

- Increased sensitivity to light, sound, touch and smell

- Hyperactivity

- Dramatic increase in sexual feelings

- Pain in the face or jaw (resembling toothache)

- Derealisation and depersonalisation

- Panic attacks

- OCD – Obsessive thoughts, which cause compulsive behaviours

- Pure O – Obsessive, inappropriate thoughts, often about sexual, homosexual, aggressive or religious thoughts, acts or beliefs

- Thoughts about existence or the universe

- Loss of interest in family, work or other life factors

- Loss of emotion – feeling removed from people

- Alcohol and/or drug abuse as self-medication

- Difficulties at work, such as holding meetings, giving presentations, etc.

- Social phobia

- Fear of dying, fear of illness, fear of doctors, fear of dentists, etc.

- Hair pulling

- Self-harming

- Eating disorders

Although these anxiety symptoms *feel* horrific and scary, the effects are mostly harmless. The word 'feel' is the key here: the anxiety symptoms experienced are just feelings; sensations of a true emotional response that have become inappropriately activated as a response to danger – even when no real danger is present. You see, anxiety is an emotion, like happiness or sadness but, because anxiety produces some fairly intense physical and emotional responses due to its 'physical' nature, the sufferer becomes trapped in a cycle of fear and anxiety symptoms.

The key is that all of these and any other symptoms experienced because of high anxiety are quickly curable but it is vital to create the structure and apply the compliance that brings about physical changes in the subconscious mind.

It's so easy for so-called professionals to over-complicate anxiety disorders. High-anxiety conditions probably form 90 per cent of the conditions they treat and without anxious people; most would have to find alternative employment.

The truth about high anxiety conditions is clear and complete recovery from them can be achieved in days but if that were to happen, an industry would be in turmoil.

The big question is this: what is better, a billion anxious people whose families, careers, fulfilment and social interaction is, sometimes permanently destroyed by the disorder or a few thousand redundant practitioners?

I believe high-anxiety conditions to be *the* most socially, emotionally and economically damaging health-related conditions in the world. I believe we are in a pandemic of anxiety that is now building into a global health disaster. I believe that the impact of all other disease fades into insignificance compared to the global damage caused by these conditions. I also believe that we cure anxiety disorders and that if everyone had access to The Linden Method, the world would be a much calmer place.

CHAPTER SIXTEEN

Twenty-four Facts to Help Release your Misconceptions

Here follows a list of facts that I would have given my eyeteeth to have known when I was anxious.

Let me be clear on one thing. Despite the fact that I refer to anxious thoughts and sensations as 'symptoms' sometimes, this is more due to the general use of this term across the medical and psychological fraternities and linguistic 'convention' than my knowledge.

These facts are not listed in order of importance.

1. Your condition, regardless of how long you have suffered, or the intensity or combination of your sensations and thoughts, is curable. I have never been party to a case in over sixteen years of someone who is incurable.

2. In over sixteen years of treating tens of thousands of anxiety sufferers of all genders, backgrounds and ethnicities, not one, *ever*, has come to any harm at the hands of their condition.

3. None of the 'symptoms' of high anxiety are symptoms because symptoms can only be manifested during illnesses as an outward expression of infection or injury. They are sensations and thoughts associated with the anxiety response, nothing more.

4. Never have myself or my staff heard of anyone with high anxiety 'symptoms' that has also developed medical conditions as a result of their anxiety.

5. Anxiety disorders do not lead to other conditions and are totally unrelated to mental illness.

6. Depression and anxiety disorder are unrelated. Clinical depression is a chemical condition and unrelated to the 'fed-up' sensations and thoughts experienced by anxiety sufferers. It is physically impossible to be clinically depressed and anxious simultaneously – it's like being happy and sad simultaneously, it just doesn't happen. In fact, anxiety and depression are at the two extremes of human emotion because depression causes a complete removal of emotional responses whereas anxiety is the most extreme manifestation of emotional experiences.

7. Panic attacks are not harmful, they are simply the body's mechanism for letting off steam when no real threat exists to fight or flee from. When adrenaline reaches a high level and is not 'used up' appropriately, the body activates a panic attack to use it up fast. While sometimes frightening and uncomfortable, panic attacks are harmless. No one has ever come to harm because of a panic attack. Like a long sneeze designed to expel foreign bodies from the nasal passages, they can cause sometimes very uncomfortable sensations but they are harmless and once this 'mental sneeze' expels unused adrenaline, the body settles back down. We provide a tool called the Panic Attack Eliminator in our programs that undermines and removes panic attacks.

8. Anxiety disorders including agoraphobia, panic disorder, OCD, Pure O and GAD are NOT illnesses, they are symptoms of high anxiety.

9. Anxiety is an emotion and just because you have too much of it right now doesn't mean you are ill. Just because fear manifests so physically and can affect your thoughts doesn't make it a mental illness; it is what it is – an emotion and given the correct guidance, it can be 'turned down' to an appropriate level; permanently.

10. Depersonalisation and derealisation are NOT disorders, they are a normal feature of high anxiety and disappear when anxiety has been reduced back to normal. Just because they make you feel so weird, unwell or scared doesn't mean they are threatening, permanent or the sign of anything more than high anxiety.

11. Pure O is NOT a separate disorder. It, like OCD, is a symptom of high anxiety caused by 'what if' notions sent out by the subconscious in order to assess risk. Whether they cause sexual, homosexual, aggressive, incestuous or other disturbing thoughts is irrelevant… the thoughts are nothing to worry about and will stop permanently when your anxiety has gone.

12. OCD is not an illness and you are not 'OCD' no one is defined by a disorder. OCD doesn't exist as far as I am concerned, however, what does exist is the mind's predisposition to carrying out risk assessments during the anxiety response, which is what causes people to carry out 'safety seeking' rituals and to obsess about those things that COULD potentially represent a risk. The only difference between OCD and agoraphobia, for example, is the subject matter.

13. Exposure therapy does not work for the treatment of high-anxiety conditions and anyone who tells you they do must be avoided. Exposure therapy MAY have short-term success but the long-term result is often worsening of the original condition and symptoms.

14. Cognitive therapy or CBT CANNOT work in the treatment of high-anxiety conditions. This isn't my opinion, it's scientific fact backed up by tens of thousands of very unsatisfied anxiety sufferers. CBT is counterproductive and inappropriate because it asks the sufferer to practise being anxious. Scientifically and psychologically the core processes and structures of CBT are based on flawed science and zero curative evidence. Just because it's free and recommended by many people around the world doesn't make it right. But don't take my word for it, ask the people who matter, the millions of people who haven't been cured by it. It doesn't take long to find them.

15. Inability to concentrate is normal during anxiety disorders as the mind resources responsible for focusing on specific tasks are re-tasked to addressing potential threat.

16. Loss of libido and/or loss or lessening of your feelings for your loved ones is common during anxiety conditions as the psychology of the brain changes in order to focus on potential threat.

17. Anxiety disorders present with myriad thoughts and sensations, which are cut and dried in terms of diagnosis. If a medical person or psychologist has diagnosed an anxiety disorder, accept it; to my knowledge none of my clients have ever been misdiagnosed.

18. Agoraphobia isn't a disorder, it's a feature of high anxiety – a symptom if you like. Agoraphobia is normal and expected safety-seeking behaviour during high anxiety and is only different to OCD or Pure O in its subject matter. Like flicking switches or hand washing, it's just a simple control device used by sufferers to prevent/control anxiety or panic attacks.

19. Your heart racing is normal in high anxiety. A racing heart won't stop. Athletes push their hearts to extremes and just because your racing heart is activated by adrenaline doesn't make the effect any more threatening.

20. Palpitations are normal and expected symptoms of the anxiety response and are not related to cardiac health. Ignore them. Never in sixteen years of helping tens of thousands of anxiety sufferers to recover has one person with palpitations come to any harm.

21. Digestive issues and incontinence are normal during high-anxiety conditions. While sometimes painful, disturbing and embarrassing, they will stop when anxiety is reduced back to a normal level.

22. Drug therapies are not curative. No one has ever developed a drug that can seek out, select and 'treat' the neural pathways responsible for the 'memory' of your inappropriately high level of the emotion of fear and administer the correct level of targeted treatment to remove ONLY your inappropriate fears without damaging or changing other areas of the brain ... it's impossible. Anti-depressants, as the name suggests, are NOT curative anxiety treatments and other drugs serve only to mask symptoms, which must, one day, be faced again.

23. There is only one cure for high-anxiety conditions. I use the term 'cure' in the widest sense of its meaning. Cures can only happen in clinical illness. Anxiety can be quickly deactivated.

24. The emotion of fear can be deactivated in milliseconds after it is used in appropriate flight-or-fight response. The only reason you still suffer is because you have become trapped in a cycle of anxiety causing risk assessments, anxiety causing symptoms, risk assessments assessing the symptoms as risk, risk is dealt with by adrenaline, adrenaline causes symptoms and anxious thoughts and so on.

Now I Want to Help You!

I CAN'T CURE YOU in this book but I can cure you.

The fast relief you can experience will inspire you, excite you and provide you with the freedom to move forwards with your life, regardless of how long you have suffered or how severe you think your issues are.

Whether you have been diagnosed with stress, anxiety, depression, agoraphobia, OCD, Pure O, health anxiety, panic disorder, PTSD, self-harming, eating disorders or any combination of these conditions, I will show you what to do now to start to feel better tomorrow.

I will also make it a very easy decision to make because if – just if – you don't feel that what I do for you hasn't helped you, you don't have to pay a single penny and it will be free, all of it –my method, my support staff, my resources, advice, reassurance and guidance. Why? Because I know that you will love what it does for you.

My recovery was down to one thing: the structured program of recovery I now call The Linden Method, the story of the development of that process is contained in this book.

If you would like to live The Linden Method and would like to get access to my team of Anxiety Recovery Specialists and all of the program materials, my staff and I will help you until you are free from the grips of your inappropriate fear.

Use the web address in the offer below and get the full Linden Method program plus, for readers of this book only, a copy of my Mentoring DVD set – saving over £59 or $98.

Our lives now exist around making sure everyone who needs it gets the support guidance and recovery they deserve and our belief is that your recovery has just started.

All our love
Charles and Beth Linden

PS. Don't ever let anyone tell you that recovery is impossible – believe it is possible because I assure you with all my heart that it is and that you will be anxiety free, happy and fulfilled.